The first thing yo ⟨MW01615440⟩ ⟨...⟩
is his genuine authenticity. While his book My Father's Son
*will make you laugh and cry at the same time, inspire and
challenge you simultaneously – what will grab you again and
again is Wayne's unvarnished transparency. That's the Wayne
Alcorn I know and love, and you will too!*

Sam Chand
International speaker, author and leadership consultant,
founder of Sam Chand Leadership Institute

*Wayne Alcorn is undoubtedly one of the finest and perhaps
most enduring spiritual leaders in the world today. I and many
others are thrilled he is finally putting his wisdom to pen. This
book* My Father's Son *is a must read for every person seeking
to flourish in today's modern world. It is the roadmap towards
a more fruitful, whole and meaningful life.*

Glen Gerreyn
Author of Men of Honour and director of The HopeFull Institute

*I have been very blessed in my life to have some great father
figures around me to help shape and guide me into the person
I have become today. Since starting out as a young 18-year-old,
Wayne Alcorn has been one of those influential father figures
that not only encouraged me, but thousands of others around
the globe.*

Andy Gourley
Founder of Redfrogs Australia

The message of this book is one that is deeply needed in this generation. Wayne has walked through this journey and now has the privilege of helping others with it. My Father's Son *will inspire you to live your life the way God intended you to. As a personal mentor and pastor of mine, I can attest to the wisdom that Wayne carries. I know that everyone who picks up this book will be profoundly impacted.*

Joel Chelliah
Author of *The Chat*, senior pastor of Centrepoint Church

'Wake up the mighty men!' This command from the prophet Joel is being echoed across the earth today. Nations need their families back. And if we are going to get our families back, we need to get our fathers back. And if we are going to get our fathers back, then we need to call them into authentic manhood and fatherhood. My Father's Son *is a momentum builder for heaven's strategy of challenging, identifying, confronting, encouraging, unlocking and releasing men into their destiny. Grateful for Pastor Wayne initiating a conversation for us as men to abandon the wounded life, disrupt fruitless cycles and set new generational norms and rhythms. Without question we need this message!*

Chris Estrada
Pastor, author, international speaker and director of Missions Me College

What a timely and powerful book My Father's Son *is. Wayne writes from his heart, his testimony and his passion – to see fathers step into walking out their godly legacy. This book is filled with wisdom that people will relate to. Relationships and their complexities are talked about honestly, with the resolute kindness of God woven throughout. I know this book will be a great blessing to whoever finds themselves reading it.*

Darlene Zschech
Australian singer, composer, worship leader, pastor and author

My Father's Son *is not just another book on fathering. Wayne Alcorn weaves together profound insights with transparent, seriously funny storytelling and practical how-tos that help you live and lead well. But* My Father's Son *is not just a book for dads. It is also very much for mums, sons and daughters seeking to understand and live fully with Dad. It's a book on God's design for your very best relationship for your very best life.*

Joel Holm
Pastor, author, teacher, podcaster and consultant

The first thing that impacted me as I read the extract of My Father's Son *by Wayne Alcorn is that it is a well-written and thoughtful work. The sort of considered wrestling with words and feelings, like a man who is committed to grow up and deal with the big issues and become who he is meant to be.*

I felt like an invited friend to a rite of passage into private places. I am grateful to have met Alex, I know Wayne better through his journey. We will all be better humans for this expedition into the Father's heart.

Robert Falzon
Founder of menALIVE, author of *Raising Fathers*
and co-author of *The Father Factor*

I have known Wayne Alcorn for the better part of 30 years. I'm going to start by saying that Wayne is the real deal. His love for his wife and his children (who are now thriving adults), has been a tremendous example to not only me, but to so many in this nation. There are so many things I could talk about, but I want to focus on his heart to see men find the love of a father and his desire to help people like me, who grew up without a dad for the better part of my life, to become better men and great dads. I have recently become a dad, and I'm thankful to have pastors, friends and mentors to guide me in this journey. It can be a challenge when you have never been shown how to be a dad because of an absent father. It's why books like this are so important. I'm also very aware of the effect it had on me growing up to not have any consistent guidance as I entered into manhood. I had a loving mum and I'm extremely grateful for her, but there is something so powerful about the affirmation of a father to his son. Enjoy the read – you will be better for it.

Jason Stevens
Former NRL player, author, TV presenter and filmmaker

WAYNE ALCORN

MY FATHER'S SON

A GENERATIONAL JOURNEY

Published by Acorn Press, an imprint of Bible Society Australia.
GPO Box 4161
Sydney NSW 2001
Australia
www.biblesociety.org.au
Charity licence 19 000 528
ACN 148 058 306

ISBN: 9780647532041 (paperback); 9780647532058 (ebook);
9780647532607 (international print edition)

 A catalogue record for this
work is available from the
National Library of Australia

Unless otherwise indicated, Scripture quotations are taken from the
Holy Bible, New International Version® Anglicised, NIV® Copyright
© 1979, 1984, 2011 by Biblica, Inc.® Used by permission. All rights
reserved worldwide. Quotations marked 'NKJV' are taken from the
New King James Version®. Copyright © 1982 by Thomas Nelson.
Used by permission. All rights reserved.

Cover design by Nathan Cahyadi.
Cover image by Anabel Litchfield.
Text design and layout by John Healy.

To my family.

Contents

Prologue

I'd like to start by introducing you to Alex.

Over the years, Alex had gained a reputation as the town drunk, well known for going on a bender and raising the roof in his hometown in outback Queensland. At the age of 24, he found himself sitting in a place that had become all too familiar – a cell in the local jail.

As Alex sat on that filthy bunkbed, he began a confronting conversation with himself. 'I've become the person I never wanted to be,' he said, as he thought about his life and what he saw as a hopeless future.

Alex also wondered what his father had thought of him. He didn't know, because he'd never been told. He was certainly never told he was loved, valued or respected.

Where were the hopes and dreams of the life Alex had imagined as a young boy? He began smoking when he was 12 years old and drinking alcohol at 14. When he was 19, his father died and, by the time he was 20, Alex was a chain-smoking alcoholic. His situation continued to deteriorate: in and out of work, always in some kind of trouble, and often in that jail.

He did remember one thing his dad had once said: 'The worst thing a man can be is a liar, a drunkard and a thief.'

Alex thought to himself, 'Well, my whole life is made up of these things' – the three things his father had told him he shouldn't be. 'Not one person in this entire town cares if I live or die,' he concluded.

In that moment, Alex began to plan how he would take his life. He gave it more thought than he had given anything in years. Having sobered up, he was released the next morning and returned to work; but all through that day, he could think about just one thing: what was the best way to end his life?

Alex lived in shared accommodation with a friend who owned a gun. That night, he decided, he would take the gun and use it on himself: even sober, it seemed the quickest way to end his misery. Alex went looking for the gun, but it wasn't there. He would find out later that it had been lent to a cousin who had gone on a hunting trip and who wasn't expected back for a few days.

Alex was frustrated. A couple of nights later, he was downtown again drinking with his mates. It was Sunday night, and he was looking to drown his sorrows and maybe have some fun. That same night, just as they did every week, a small bunch of Christians gathered outside the local café. They presented a predictable program: some people would share their personal stories of faith, and a small choir would sing. It provided great entertainment for the mocking crowd, and Alex had often been one of the hecklers.

That night, it was the same crowd, the same songs, the same choir; but this time it was going to be different. Something moved Alex to respond to the message of hope.

Alex's heavenly Father stepped in. And his life changed forever.

This book tells part of Alex's remarkable story – and mine. You see, Alex is my father.

PART 1

The Father Wound

Introduction

I remember the day clearly. We were almost at the end of the twentieth century. A brand-new millennium was at our doorstep. There were all kinds of predictions about the change that awaited all of us. The Doomsday prophets were having a field day. Ah yes, who can forget 'Y2K'? It's amazing that we're all still here!

Late in 1999, I was sitting in the front of a church, about to speak on a Sunday morning, knowing that the seasons of life were also changing for me personally. I'd been leading a program in our nation called Youth Alive.

It had been an amazing ride: from being a local youth group leader in a regional town to seeing our desire to help young people unfold. Youth Alive became a significant force for good, helping countless thousands of young people in our nation. Beyond that, it played a part in shaping the contemporary Australian church.

In that moment, I heard what I believe was the whisper of heaven into my own heart: 'You've spent the last 20 years helping young people. Now it's time to help their fathers help them.'

Since then, I've spent much of my time talking to and with men – at church, at camps, at conferences and at men's events. There have been conversations in boardrooms, over barbecues in backyards, on fishing trips and in the grandstands at sporting events, both large and small.

One moment stands out. I was in the far north of my state, in the beautiful tropical region of Queensland, to speak at another men's event. The men there were ordinary guys who loved outdoor activities – sport, recreational fishing, camping and the like – and they were the kind of people I love hanging with. There was a broad range of age groups. Professional businessmen rubbed shoulders with tradesmen, middle management and retirees. Many were husbands. A lot were fathers. Some were single. But we all had a common need. (Read on: you'll discover it!)

My goal that day was to inspire men in their journey through life. In one of the sessions, I showed a video about the extraordinary story of Dick Hoyt and his son Rick, who had cerebral palsy. Rick loved sport and, after he graduated from college, he and Dick entered a fun run together. In the years that followed, Team Hoyt competed in over 1000 races, including 32 Boston Marathons.

In 1989, officials granted special permission for Dick and Rick to participate in the Hawaiian Ironman. It's a gruelling course. To add to the challenge, Dick had not long recovered from a heart condition, but they were determined to race. Dick towed his son in a boat in the 3.8 kilometre swim. He cycled 180 kilometres with Rick on the front of his bike. And he ran, pushing his son 42.2 kilometres in a wheelchair. They completed the race in just under 14.5 hours.

When the video concluded, I asked the crowd, 'I wonder how many of us here today, with our strong physiques (I took the liberty of including myself in that description) would be prepared to give all that up – even exchange places with Rick

Hoyt – in order to know, for the first time in our lives, the authentic love of our father?'

The reaction of many of the men present was amazing. Tears flowed down suntanned faces as men across that auditorium came to terms with something that had been missing in their lives for such a long time – the love of a father.

That missing love causes real pain – a 'father wound'. I've seen it in countless men since that day in the tropics so many years ago. It has been a significant part of my mission and my passion to help heal that wound. Somebody once said that if people don't know what your passion is, you probably don't have one. This book reflects mine.

I am not an academic. I am not a doctor or a psychologist. I am not a counsellor. I am, however, a pastor, a son, a father and a grandfather who wants to see men succeed in life. I've had the honour of listening to many adult men as they have shared their stories with me, and I've been entrusted with the details of painful parts of their lives. Some of these stories are included in this book, with their permission. Perhaps you have a similar story of your own? When we share our stories, we not only begin to heal ourselves, but give permission to others to share, to be vulnerable, to heal.

There is a father wound that lies deep within us all, but we don't have to stumble through life crippled by that wound or numbing the pain through unhealthy activities.

This book is an invitation to take a journey – one I hope you will take. As you read it, I trust you will become aware that there are times on that journey when we all need help that transcends human ability. We need an intervention of the Divine. I pray you will make discoveries, as you read, that will lead you to the heart of a loving, heavenly Father.

Be encouraged. There is hope. Though we will address some confronting issues in the following pages, we will also discover that with God's help, broken hearts can be healed and fractured relationships restored. There's a brighter future to be embraced for your family and the following generations through his promise:

> And he will turn
> The hearts of the fathers to the children,
> And the hearts of the children to their fathers …
>
> (Malachi 4:6 NKJV)

1. The Empty Chair

A pastor friend shared with me about a time he interviewed some men as part of a Father's Day church service. He asked them to share a favourite memory of their dad, a defining moment. He began by sharing his own: as a young boy, he drove interstate with his father to watch Australia's iconic Bathurst 1000 motor race.

Then it was the interviewees' turn. There were funny stories, insights, and for some, heartwarming recollections of time with fathers.

For others, however, it was different. One man simply froze, tears welling up in his eyes. Then he took a deep breath and said, 'I just don't have one.'

Many other men will say the same thing. The family without a father is, sadly, all too common today. Never in the history of our nation – and, I suspect, of the Western world – have there been more children growing up with a single parent – and, most likely, an absent father.[1]

Ultimately, relationships, families and communities are affected by the deficit in the human soul that results from that very real and painful void, the absence of the father. This father wound cuts deep in generations and individuals.

There's an empty chair at the family table. And it leaves a void in the lives of the women and children who struggle to adapt and function as best they can around it. Take Julie, an incredible, godly woman who is raising her son on her own. She described her fears and concerns to me:

It's really hard not having a male influence or father figure in my son's life. My biggest fear is that my son will grow up not having that someone to look up to, or to show him the way. I've always wondered, how will I show him the love of our heavenly Father if he doesn't have an example of an earthly father? How do I show him how to respect women? How do I show him how to have healthy relationships?

I've encountered many men who were raised in fatherless families. There are times when that chair at the family table is empty through no-one's fault. It is just a result of our mortality: people die, and that loss is very real and painful for their loved ones. On the other hand, fathers who choose to leave cause deep emotional scars in their children, and no doubt in their own souls as well.

Sam's story
'I don't think he loves us anymore.'

Dad 'left' us between my ages of 11 and 14. Initially he was gone a night or two, until he finally exited our family completely, with somebody who wasn't my mother.

When I was 13, I remember playing cricket in the backyard, and my mother was looking out the window as she prepared dinner … I said, 'Mum, where's Dad these days?' And then came the most negative response I have ever heard from her. She didn't turn around. She just said, 'I don't think he loves us anymore.'

Up until that time, I had been coming first at everything, then all of a sudden, I was coming last at everything. I had to cope with the fact that Dad never watched me play sport, even though I made representative teams. He didn't even attend my wedding.

As a teenager, Sam developed a wild temper after his father left. Similarly, from an early age, Paul struggled with self-esteem and acceptance due to the 'empty chair' in his life …

Paul's story
'I feel I'm less than human. I'm alien.'

My father was gone before my second birthday. Then the 'shared parenting experience' began. For the next 12 years I would be dropped at a train station late on Friday afternoons to meet my father, and would usually stay with him for the next 36 hours. For a long time, the visit mainly involved playing a lot of video games. We struggled to connect.

My mother remarried when I was 11 years old. My stepdad appeared to love my mum so much, but he didn't seem to have the capacity to love me as well. Then the verbal and mental abuse started. To protect me, my mum packed our bags and we left home in a hurry one day. That second marriage ended after less than three years.

I longed for a normal family life. We had no happy memories. Neither my biological father nor the man who was my stepfather for a short time showed me love. Any interaction I had with them seemed to come from a sense of obligation on their part. I have very little contact with either man now, but I'm left with lingering questions: Where were you? Why did you?

Like so many others, Paul carries the scars of a fatherless life. He told me that he did not feel accepted by other children his age when he was growing up. He was depressed and had suicidal thoughts. To cope with the reality of his home life, he isolated himself and slept a lot. He learned to mask his pain in public.

Paul now realises that his father had also received no love or validation from his own father. Without a father figure himself, he just did not know how to be a father, or how to love his son. In reality, we learn to be a father through being a son. What we learn we pass on.

Relationships, families and communities are all affected by the father wound, the scar left in the human soul by the painful void caused by the absence of the father. This wound cuts deep, and it can become a cycle that is repeated in future generations of fathers and sons.

We will see, however, that there can also be pain and dysfunction when the father is at home.

2. Painful Memories

Some years ago, we invited participants in a men's retreat to write letters to their fathers. Each man was given a pen, a piece of paper and a stamped envelope. For the guys whose fathers had passed away, we encouraged them to still write a letter, expressing the things they would like to have said.

I took the opportunity to write to my dad, too. It wasn't hard. I thanked him for his love, encouragement and support throughout my life. I was living in the wake of his transformed life. Others around me also seemed to be writing freely.

There were a few, however, who were obviously struggling. They had no words, and no fond memories of their fathers. One man threw down his pen and stormed out of the room. It was tough to watch. The task had taken him to a dark place of extremely painful memories.

Some of the stories in this chapter are quite graphic in their detail – specifically, those shared by Terry and Gary, who grew up experiencing extreme physical and emotional violence. I'm grateful to these brave men who have given me permission to share their stories.

Scott's story
'Dad was a stranger who only brought me sad memories.'

Scott's father suffered from a mental illness. Somehow, everyone in the family knew that. Scott certainly did, even from a very early age.

It was the 1970s, when electric shock therapy used to treat serious mental illness had adverse side effects on many who received it. In the case of Scott's father, he seemingly lost any ability to show love.

His father would also demean Scott's mother and attempt to control her by withholding the finances necessary for the day-to-day running of the family.

When they could put up with the situation no longer, an 11-year-old Scott, his mum and his brothers left the family home while his father was at work.

Scott recalls, 'Dad would come around occasionally to our new place. Rarely was that a positive time for us. Most of his visits would usually involve him lecturing us about what was wrong with Mum.'

When he was 18, Scott had to physically remove his father from their house and they didn't speak again for over five years.

'I couldn't even allow my father to come to my wedding. It wouldn't have been fair to my mother. She was the one who had sacrificed so much for my brothers and me to ensure we got a quality education. Dad was a stranger who only brought me sad memories.'

Terry's story
'Our family learned to live in fear.'

I grew up in a violent home. My earliest memories are of my father being violent towards Mum … His standard response to any situation was to throw and smash things. That included people. Once my sister had her nose broken for spending too long on the telephone. She required corrective surgery to be able to breathe properly again.

He would throw hot cups of coffee at us, along with dinner plates or anything else within range. He had been a champion boxer in his youth, and he was always quick with a right hook or an upper cut.

Our family lived in fear. We actually knew by the sound of his walk what mood he was in. We knew by the way he dropped his knife and fork onto his dinner plate when to find somewhere to hide. And hiding is what I learned to do best.

From three years old I'd learned to hide under our house and not make a sound. By the age of five, I'd developed the habit of completely freezing when anything bad happened. I didn't know what love and connection were. I had no confidence.

By the time I started school, I was traumatised and depressed, numb with shock and always emotionally exhausted. I couldn't concentrate in school and I was a prime target for bullies.

Countless times throughout my school life, I just stood there being punched or lay there being kicked, having some sort of weird out-of-body experience. It was like I was witnessing it happen to someone else. This made me a target for other predators too. When I was 10, a trusted figure began to sexually abuse me ... and I just froze in fear. The very first time it happened, I went home and told my dad. He looked at me with pure disgust and backhanded me across the face, saying, 'What the hell did you let him do that for?'

When we left the house, we'd all pretend everything was fine – we looked like the happiest family ever! Our dad was the best guy around and everyone loved him ... except us.

Gary's story

'We had to put a wardrobe and a chest of drawers against the door to keep my father out.'

I grew up afraid and insecure most of the time, never knowing what state my father would be in on his return home. This was compounded by the fact that I felt responsibility for my older brother Michael, who was born with Down syndrome. I just remember thinking, even as a child, that somehow I needed to protect him in this volatile situation.

There were rare occasions when my father was nice, but mostly he was distant – in the room but emotionally absent – then suddenly drunk and seriously angry.

Early on, I learned not to trust him. His word was never his bond. Whenever he promised to be home, he would always be hours late and usually drunk.

I can remember being locked in a room to keep me out of the firing line. Sometimes we had to put a wardrobe and a chest of drawers against the door to keep my father out.

Then one terrible day, my dad attacked my older brother. The violence was so bad that our next door neighbours intervened. I remember that night, as a young child, trying to find somewhere to sit or sleep that had not been splashed with blood.

My father went to Alcoholics Anonymous for a while but our hopes were short-lived. He continued to go downhill due to his alcoholism, until one fateful day when he attacked our neighbour with an iron bar. Looking out the window, I watched our neighbour grab that iron bar and beat my father's head in. This is something no child should ever see.

My father staggered into our house and my mother called an ambulance. By then, we didn't care if he lived or died. We just wanted peace and safety.

These stories give us an insight into the intense family violence that happens in so many homes. In many cases, it is a systematic pattern of men ruling by fear to exercise power and control over their wives and children.

While bruises and broken bones may heal for those who've experienced physical violence, the psychological scars remain and can sabotage their entire lives. In the words of a friend of mine, 'Time alone doesn't heal. It just pushes the pain deeper.' Raising these issues and talking about them will undoubtedly be painful, but it is important that we are intentional about resolving our past, about healing our father wounds.

For believers, it can be comforting to know that Jesus also experienced almost unimaginable pain. The pain inflicted on him leading up to and during his crucifixion was immense. I've watched portrayals in productions such as *The Passion of the Christ*. It's hard to watch.

His back was torn open by a cruel whip.

His head was pierced by a crown of thorns.

His side was opened by a soldier's spear.

But I wonder whether anything compared with the isolation and sense of abandonment he experienced in his final moments on the cross, as revealed in his words 'My God, my God, why have you forsaken me?' (Matthew 27:46).

The anguish of separation from his Father added to the physical pain. He wasn't disappointed by his Father, but he did feel very alone. Through that experience, we have further evidence of his humanity, which in turn gives us greater confidence that he can relate to us and we can relate to him.

3. Missing in Action

I was only a few steps from the door into a large auditorium full of teenagers. The place was alive, and a brilliant band was about to take the stage. I would be up next, to encourage young people to accept the invitation of Jesus to follow him. I felt privileged to be part of this exciting event.

Then my phone rang. It was my son, calling to tell me about an important hockey game he had played earlier that day. His team had won. He'd even scored the winning goal. I told him how happy I was.

But he wasn't as buoyant as you would expect, after tasting such success. 'Yeah, Dad. It's great. The only problem is that you weren't there.'

It was confronting to hear this from my son. I never wanted to be that guy.

For years I watched fathers drop their children off to sport or other activities. Many never watched their kids participate. Others sat and watched, but they were quite obviously uninterested – consumed with other things. I had a personal policy to be fully present wherever I was. Yet now I was at risk of becoming just like them – well-intentioned … just not present.

Mike's story

'I was angry that he missed so much of my childhood.'

Mike was the son of a famous politician. His father was very popular, and everyone in the community knew that he was always willing to help them. He was a good guy. There was just one problem: he was never home.

What breaks Mike's heart is that his dad was available to everyone – except him.

'He was just never there. If he was home, he would be on the phone, day and night.

'Every young man needs to hear their dad say "I believe in you". It's so important, but sadly, for me that's just a vacuum in my life.

'It's taken decades for me to resolve it, and with God's help I have, but I think I carried resentment for way too long. I was angry that he missed so much of my childhood. I don't remember him ever being present at any activity or sport that I participated in. He was barely even there on our family holidays.'

Mike is committed to ensuring that this is not repeated with his children and it shows.

I've watched grown men fall apart emotionally as they recall how their fathers were not around for important seasons in their lives. Perhaps their dads were off doing some important thing, yet the really important person – their son – had been left without their presence for extended periods of time. Dad was missing in action and nobody could replace him.

I know kids who never mention their dad, yet he lives with them. These fathers may be great financial providers and give their family practical support, thinking 'I'm doing my job', but in reality, they are emotionally distant.

We were sold a lie in the late twentieth century. We were told that the digital revolution would mean that we would work less and play more.

You've probably noticed that with smartphones, if we're not careful, we are never 'off'. We have our office in our back pocket. Phone calls, texts and those wretched emails can keep coming if we don't create boundaries in our lives. And our work becomes the enemy to our children.

A father who is missing in action leaves a void in his child's life. For some children, that space can be filled in healthy ways with the help of other family members and positive support structures such as youth programs, schools and sports clubs. But that void can also welcome in more negative influences. Undesirable friends and damaging behaviours can fill that need for engagement and attention.

This was the case for my own father, Alex Alcorn. Born in 1927, a time sandwiched between the First World War and the Great Depression, he suffered the loss of his mother as an infant and the brokenness of his father who was a returned soldier. Men of his father's generation, physically and emotionally wrecked by the war and the Depression, weren't renowned communicators. His father lived with a broken heart following the breakdown of his marriage, endured the pain of divorce, and experienced the death of a young wife followed by the loss of a baby son. It couldn't have been easy for him. Alex recognised that.

Dad didn't often speak about his childhood, but I recall one conversation in which he shared his heart about his father (my grandfather):

My father wasn't affectionate, but he was a well-meaning man. He showed me that on a few occasions, by lending a helping hand when I was in trouble. It meant a lot that he would come out and play cricket with my brother and me, but through all my childhood, I didn't feel like he wanted to be with me. That sense of rejection had a lasting impact on me. Possibly the most damaging effect of all was a deep sense of inferiority that I carried for many years.

Filling that void

It doesn't matter who we are: everyone wants to belong and be loved. I shared that thought over lunch with a recently retired Navy Seal, who wholeheartedly agreed with me. During the conversation, he told me how much he missed that life now that it was over.

I was keen to know what it was he missed the most. Was it the pay and conditions? No. The skills he developed? No. There's lots of cool equipment to play with, but that wasn't it either. Nor was it the travel around the globe.

'Family,' he said, fighting back the tears. 'It's the sense of family. The bond you build with people that have your back every day of your life is something you never forget.'

And people who are lacking in family support will try to fill the void in other ways. An Australian military chaplain I spoke to believes there are two main reasons young men join the army:

- Their parents make them sign up, because they believe that the system will equip them with skills and teach them discipline. They hope that the military structure, along with the relational dynamics they'll experience, will help their son become a better human.

- Their family is a mess, and this is seen as the best way to escape.

Some of you may be familiar with a well-known story about a little boy who asked his exhausted father one night how much he earned per hour.[2] The man was a little surprised to hear a question like that from someone so young, but he gave him an answer.

Sometime later, the boy returned and asked for a loan of some money. This angered the overworked dad, so he sent his son to his room. Feeling remorseful, the father eventually went in to see if his son was still awake and apologise for his reaction.

He entered the room and spoke much more softly this time. 'I've been thinking, maybe I was too hard on you earlier,' said the man. 'It's been a long day and I took my frustration out on you. Here's the money you asked for.'

The little boy sat up beaming and thanked his father. Then he reached under his pillow and pulled out his savings, which he began to count out.

'Why do you need more money if you already had this much?' the father asked.

'Because I didn't have enough before … but I do now!' cried the little boy. 'So can I please buy an hour of your time? Please come home early tomorrow, because I would like to have dinner with you.'

The void left by the empty chair can cause people to explore ways to numb the pain – and sadly, this path often leads them to further harm.

4. Numbing the Pain

After our Sunday church services, people queue up to get their morning coffee. One week, when I was chatting with those in the queue, one lady asked if I would pray with her. She seemed distressed. When she told me her story, I understood why. A few hours earlier she'd had a conversation with her son, Vince, that would break any mother's heart. The young man lived interstate and was in considerable trouble with the police.

'My son is an ice addict,' she said. 'He's destroying his life … and he's causing great pain for our family. He's angry all the time.'

Before we prayed, I asked her if she knew why he was angry. 'Was it the drugs?' I asked.

'Not really,' she replied through tears. 'He came to a point in his life where he was furious that he grew up without a dad. Things have been out of control ever since.'

There are many men like Vince – young men who are turning to substance abuse in an attempt to fill the vacuum left by the father who was absent from their lives.

Trapped by addictions

I had the privilege of interviewing a doctor who specialises in the treatment of people trapped by drug addiction. (Due to the sensitivities of his work, I won't identify him.) In the course of his work, he helps his patients deal with various aspects of drug dependency – including withdrawal symptoms, overdoses and mental illness.

Many of his patients share a common reason for turning to drugs in the first place. He explained that it is 'to take away their emotional and psychological pain. Narcotics leave them feeling euphoric for a while. A user does not really care whether they live or die. Their primary goal is to reach ... a place of peace in their traumatic life.'[3] They are human souls trying to find something to sedate the pain within.

The majority of his patients come from broken homes with little family structure. His observation is backed up by numerous studies on the effects of family structure on tobacco, alcohol and drug use. Of his patients:

- Very few had a biological father living with them.
- Many had poor role models in their life, causing them to gravitate to 'the wrong crowd' and engage in delinquent behaviour.
- Many were neglected, and it was common for their mother to have had a number of partners cycle through their home during their childhood.
- Many were abused from a young age, the resulting trauma leading to recurring feelings of shame and emotional pain.
- Many had committed crimes to support their habit. Many had resorted to stealing. A lot had become drug dealers. Some had turned to prostitution.

It's not only illegal drugs that cause ongoing damage. Alcohol also destroys many lives. Andy Gourley (aka 'Boss Frog'), founder and director of Red Frogs Australia, set up that organisation to help young people navigate and resist Australia's culture of excessive drinking.[4] Red Frogs is now a global phenomenon. I asked Andy, 'Where do you think the need to drink starts with young people?' He believes one of the key factors is parental role modelling:

> When we visit the home of young people with an emerging drinking problem, we quickly see where it has started. There's a pattern of irresponsible behaviour with alcohol in the family, and the kids are merely copying it. Often there is no one at home to provide clear boundaries and hold their children accountable for their actions.

Terry's story (continued)
'I was depressed whenever I was sober.'

By 11, I had severe anxiety and depression. I was on autopilot like a zombie. I couldn't function or bond with other people. I wasn't doing schoolwork and I wasn't able to explain myself. The school knew there was a problem and spoke to my mum. They sent me to doctors, psychologists, psychiatrists and paediatricians. I spent a whole year with people assessing me to find out what was wrong.

But in our family we didn't tell the truth. We didn't trust others, so no-one spoke up. I was not capable of articulating my issues and I certainly wasn't capable of honesty. I was frozen and in pain. I wanted to die. I'd often look in the mirror, hating myself, wishing I was dead.

I couldn't sleep, so at night-time, I would drink wine from my parents' fridge until I felt sleepy. I didn't break the habit of drinking myself to sleep for many years.

By my teenage years I was smoking pot. By my twenties, I was dulling the pain by snorting cocaine and staying out drinking until sunrise and then sleeping it off.

I was depressed whenever I was sober, which meant I wasn't often sober. I'd learned my whole life to hide – so that's what I did. I hid behind drugs, booze and a facade of success. Amid the storm of trauma and pain, I managed to get a job as a manager of a large retailer. I was making okay money, but spending it all on drugs and booze.

The effect of absent fathers is also seen in adolescent sexual behaviour. The Fathering Project notes that 'the odds of increased sexual risk behaviours or teenage pregnancy are lowest when fathers are present throughout childhood.'[5] These behaviours are increased for children 'with fathers who are disengaged or provide inadequate support in early life.'[6]

Pornography is another way boys and men attempt to numb the pain. Pornography offers a fantasy world, filled with empty promises and the lure of extreme and exaggerated passion. But it's completely devoid of the very thing men crave – intimacy.

The most serious effect of pornography is in relationships, which are damaged through this addictive behaviour. We hurt the people who are closest to us – wives, fiancées, girlfriends – who feel violated. As one counsellor said to a group of men gathered to discuss this issue, 'Making love is about your partner. Porn is all about you.'

Ultimately, we hurt ourselves when it comes to addictions. Guilt (*what I've done*) turns into shame (*what I've become*). We then distance ourselves from our loved ones, hoping they never discover the failure we feel we've become.

When we are tempted to withdraw from our family, friends and community, it is important to remind ourselves that we are all human. All men, regardless of age or social status, can struggle with this stuff, Christians included. It is possible to love Christ with all your heart and yet be wrestling with addictions.

The apostle Paul himself reflected on the very human struggle we all face when it comes to unhelpful behaviours:

> I do not understand what I do. For what I want to do I do not do, but what I hate I do … For I have the desire to do what is good, but I cannot carry it out. For I do not do the good I want to do, but the evil I do not want to do – this I keep on doing (Romans 7:15, 18b–19).

I'm not suggesting that Paul was struggling with addictive behaviours, but I want you to know that you are not alone, no matter what you may be struggling with. The critical thing to note is that there is help available to you.

All of the men who shared their stories as I prepared this book are of mature age now. They are thriving in life, but that didn't happen by accident. It's only because they discovered the pathway to wholeness – the love of their heavenly Father:

> I sought the LORD, and he answered me;
> he delivered me from all my fears.
> Those who look to him are radiant;
> their faces are never covered with shame (Psalm 34:4–5).

PART 2

The Father's Heart

Introduction

People don't set out to be alcoholics or drug addicts. It's what happens when we look to the wrong things to give us comfort, to medicate our pain and brokenness. Just like Alex Alcorn did.

Alex's life was dark and seemingly helpless after his father died. At the age of 24, Alex felt empty and purposeless, and suicide seemed a real option. Having consumed a lot of alcohol, he and his friends were in town heckling the 'Come to Jesus' group who were preaching in the street that Sunday night in September 1951.

The preacher that evening had one simple truth to share – a truth straight from the words of Jesus: 'If the Son sets you free, you will be free indeed' (John 8:36).

When he was finished, he climbed down from the back of the truck on which he had been standing, and the little choir began to sing a classic old hymn. The chorus went as follows: 'Come home, come home; you who are weary come home.'[1] Those words hit Alex hard, cutting through his drunken state, straight through his heart. 'Come home,' he thought to himself. 'Why don't I?'

And so, still very drunk and without shoes or a shirt, Alex began to stagger forward. As he approached that group of Christians, his friends thought he was going to cause trouble – pick a fight, maybe. They were totally unprepared for what happened next.

Alex stopped walking and dropped to his knees, down in the gutter. One gentleman from the Christian group approached and touched him on the shoulder. 'Would you like to pray the sinner's prayer?'

Alex didn't know what that was, but he did know that he wanted to say something to God. 'I don't even know if you are real, up there,' he said, looking up to the night sky. 'But if you are, just do one thing … help me get up sober, and I will believe in you for the rest of my life.'

And he did!

The local police sergeant was so excited that Alex Alcorn had found religion that he went up to him, hugged him and thanked him for making such a wonderful decision. I suspect that he was also hoping he'd have a little less work to do.

As a result of that simple prayer, Alex Alcorn became a new man – living proof of what the apostle Paul wrote in 2 Corinthians 5:17: 'Therefore, if anyone is in Christ, he is a new creation; old things have passed away; behold, all things have become new' (NKJV).

The pain and dysfunction didn't go away immediately. It never does. Though we are forgiven for our past in an instant, the challenge remains to live out our faith daily. We learn that this is possible, because the Holy Spirit helps us navigate an exciting new life. When Alex stood up on that Sunday night, he began a journey, walking with the Lord, which continued for the next 70 years. He had discovered the Father's heart.

5. God ... My Dad?

It's going to be hard to call God 'Father' if your view of father-hood has been distorted by negative experiences with your earthly father. There will always be a struggle to connect with a living and loving God if you see him as harsh, distant or absent. So many men tell me this is one of the greatest challenges in their life.

This isn't just a modern phenomenon, though. It's been a challenge for people throughout human history. There is a well-known prayer recorded in the Gospels by both Matthew and Luke. It is usually referred to as 'The Lord's Prayer', but at the risk of being controversial, I'd like to suggest that it could easily be termed 'The Disciples' Prayer'.

There are many prayers of Jesus recorded in the Bible. The longest is found in John 17. But in the prayer known as the Lord's Prayer, he shows his followers how to pray. We are shown how to make requests for the things we need, both practical and spiritual.

Perhaps the key aspect of the entire prayer, however, is found in the first line: 'Our *Father*'. What an amazing concept Jesus was teaching his disciples – 'You can talk to Dad, and when you do, you can be confident that he hears you.'

Let's go to this special moment in Jesus' ministry:

One day Jesus was praying in a certain place. When he finished, one of his disciples said to him, 'Lord, teach us to pray, just as John taught his disciples' (Luke 11:1).

What the disciple was saying is this: 'Hey, we saw you inter-acting with the Creator of the universe. Please show us how to connect with him too.' Read on …

> He said to them, 'When you pray, say:
> "Father,
> hallowed be your name,
> your kingdom come.
> Give us each day our daily bread.
> Forgive us our sins,
> for we also forgive everyone who sins against us.
> And lead us not into temptation"' (Luke 11:2–4).

The rather formal words 'Father, hallowed be your name' can make God sound stern, austere and distant – until we take a closer look. The original Greek word used here is 'Abba'. The equivalent word in our modern English is 'Daddy'. It conveys love and affection, not just strength and power.

The disciples were Jews, and they would have been familiar with many of the names used to address God, such as:

- *Elohim* – 'God of strength and power'
- *Jehovah* – 'the eternal and absolute source of everything'
- *Adonai* – 'lord' or 'master'.

But here, to their amazement, was Jesus telling them to call God 'Father', or 'Daddy'. That would have blown their minds! It's an extraordinary concept, but for some people it's also a distressing one. I wonder what relationship each of the 12 disciples had with his own father and how that affected how each disciple heard what Jesus was telling him.

I wonder what your experience has been.

In Part 1 of this book, you read stories from men who have experienced the absence of a father through separation, premature death or divorce, or because the father was there but preoccupied by work or other obsessions. Maybe he was struggling with issues himself.

So when we come to the Lord's Prayer, and are encouraged to call God 'Father', it's common to find that some men and women project those negative images onto God, often unconsciously.

Then, making things worse, these images have been reinforced in the hearts of many people through their exposure to dead religion. It's cold and irrelevant and presents God as angry, distant and out of touch with our needs.

It does not present him as warm, tenderhearted or desirous of relationship with us.

Please understand that dead religion is not true Christianity. Rather, it acts like spiritual immunisation, where we get a small dose of the real thing – or even worse, a synthetic version. It will inoculate you, and it may prevent you from ever experiencing an authentic relationship with God.

I've met a lot of people who think that God is an angry, harsh judge. This was reinforced for them in church settings where the preaching was full of rules and regulations, and lacking love and affection. Yet again, this is a poor representation of a God who is a gracious Father, wanting relationship with his children.

Perhaps you have also had a bad experience in church. Maybe you were misunderstood, or maybe you were just bored silly. I am sorry for that, because you have missed out on a church that is a true reflection of a loving, creative God.

My hope for you, if you are one of those people who've 'checked out' of church, is that you will reconsider who God really is – a loving Father who wants a personal relationship with you. There are so many churches that present a life-giving message in communities where you will feel welcome and accepted.

Remember Scott from chapter 2? Here are his thoughts on seeing God as our loving Father:

> My father was an authoritarian and controlling figure, who would quote verses from the Bible and weaponise them.

Scott's father was eventually diagnosed with a mental illness. Although this helps explain his bizarre behaviour, the reality is that it caused their family home to be a dark place, filled with fear. How sad, when God's word is meant to be a source of light and joy.

Scott went on to become a Christian, but even then, he struggled with talking to the Father. Scott reflects:

> When I pray, I'm comfortable talking to Jesus as my Lord. I know he's our intercessor. I get the Trinity, so I know he'll talk to the Father. I think I'm a lot like other men, who would prefer to talk to Jesus than address the Father.

Having heard his story, we can understand why; but Jesus helps us not to be afraid of or distant from our Father God. In his teaching us to pray, he is also leading us to him.

I love watching a father tenderly embrace his child. That's a picture of Abba Father: gentle, affirming and protective. That's the view of God that Jesus was showing his followers: one who is ever present. One who is just, merciful and kind.

He is one whom I can trust. He's generous, welcoming and forgiving – and he listens to those who call on him.

In the biblical records of his earthly ministry, it becomes obvious that Jesus' purpose was to show us the Father – and the Father's heart – and bring us home.

Here's the other version of the 'Lord's Prayer' that we find in the Bible, recorded by Matthew:

Our Father in heaven,
hallowed be your name,
your kingdom come,
your will be done,
   on earth as it is in heaven.
Give us today our daily bread.
And forgive us our debts,
   as we also have forgiven our debtors.
And lead us not into temptation,
   but deliver us from the evil one (Matthew 6:9–13).

6. Homecoming

At high school, and in my tertiary studies, I majored in the sciences. I had this lofty plan of becoming a marine biologist, floating around the Great Barrier Reef and being paid for it! While that plan came and went, I still remember one particular (and rather peculiar) physics lecturer and his lesson on Newton's Third Law of Motion: 'For every action there is an equal and opposite reaction.'

A similar principle applies to life. For every decision there is a consequence. We can't change our past, but we can change our future, based on the decisions we make today. We are, in fact, the product of every decision we make.

Let me illustrate with a story about a son that we can all identify with. He's the central character in one of the best-known stories in the Bible – the story of the prodigal son. You can find it in Luke chapter 15.

The son of a wealthy father on a large estate asked his father for his inheritance early and then left to travel the world. He made bad choice after bad choice, spending his money on wine and women, on late nights and 'good times'. He soon burned through his inheritance, and when his money ran out, so did his friends. Alone and desperately hungry, he was forced to find work feeding pigs and sharing their food.

He was a long way from home.

Life was not meant to be like this, he thought. Even the lowly servants in his father's house fared better. He made a decision:

'I will set out and go back to my father and say to him: Father, I have sinned against heaven and against you. I am no longer worthy to be called your son; make me like one of your hired servants' (Luke 15:18–19).

The son didn't for a moment think he would receive his father's forgiveness. He expected recrimination for his decisions; at best, he hoped for a servant's job on his father's estate. The story continues:

So he got up and went to his father. But while he was still a long way off, his father saw him and was filled with compassion for him; he ran to his son, threw his arms around him and kissed him (Luke 15:20).

Just pause for a moment and imagine the scene. It's incredible! The son could never have imagined the welcome he would receive.

His dad *ran* towards him. In that culture, mature-aged men did not run, let alone wealthy, powerful men. It was undignified. It simply wasn't done. But reputation mattered little to this father in that moment. He considered nothing more important than his desire to show the great love he felt for his son who had come home.

The reunion was powerful: no finger-pointing – just open arms. The young man had been with pigs. To the father, who was a Jew, his son would have been unclean on so many levels. Despite all that, he just kissed him. Why? The love for his son trumped everything!

The son had rehearsed his apology, but love covered his misdemeanours. The father didn't even raise the subject of his sin. He didn't ask where he'd been. He didn't call him 'rebel', 'sinner' or 'prodigal'. Did you know that the word 'prodigal' isn't even in Scripture? It seems that we are the ones who give labels.

Instead of punishment, there were presents. The father ordered that a robe, a ring and new sandals be placed upon his son. All three items are significant:

- The *robe* covered his filthy condition.
- The *ring* was a statement that his authority in the family had been restored.
- The *sandals* affirmed his identity and status as his father's son, because servants weren't given these – only sons.

I've read this parable many times. Almost every time I sense a longing within for people everywhere, and broken men in particular, to discover a God like this. Not a mystical, impersonal force in the sky. Not a harsh disciplinarian. A personal loving Father – still searching for his sons.

The Bible is more relevant today than you can imagine: the parable of the prodigal son continues to play out in so many men's lives.

Shane's story

'I had two motivations in life: to get money and to get girls.'

My parents were pastors, so church was our whole life. Growing up, home was safe, uncomplicated and nurturing. At the age of nine, I made Jesus my best friend. But as I moved into my teen years, an internal voice that simply wanted to be accepted got louder.

Attention from friends and the fear of missing out became my drivers in high school. I started doing silly things to get a reaction from peers. By the time I had left home and was at university, it became partying, chasing good times and craving life's pleasures.

After university, I had two motivations in life: to get money and to get girls. Life for me was about what I could get out of it. I still believed in God, but he was very far down my list of important things.

Next to the deep internal voice that was crying out for acceptance was another voice that quietly whispered, 'One day you'll get back to all that church stuff.' I shrugged it off, thinking I would be the one who would determine when that 'one day' would be.

In the early months of 2015 I started to ask myself big life questions: 'What's beyond the universe? How do I know there's a God? Do I think there's a God because I was brainwashed as a child?' Then I went to church with my sister for the first time in a long time.

That night I had a powerful encounter with God. From within me, I heard God's voice tell me that he loved me. In a moment, God flooded my heart with his love. Every craving of my heart was satisfied. All the 'getting' of life was quenched. I had reconnected with Jesus Christ.

Every day since then, I wake up knowing that I am fully loved and accepted, and that no matter the circumstances, Jesus is with me.

The parable of the prodigal son is the story of Shane, and the story of all humanity. Even though we may have once known God and then chosen to go our own way, he is waiting to welcome us home, no matter how far off-track we have wandered.

I've known many men who've watched their sons turn their backs on God and separate themselves from his family.

I was once one of those 'prodigals'.

Peer pressure. Insecurities. My own journey of discovery. They all contributed to me drifting from faith. God, however, was always there.

Some friends invited me to a Christian concert when I was about 17. The artist was Andraé Crouch. It was quite a show. The musicianship of the band was captivating. But deep down I knew there was something more than excellent musicians and an enjoyable performance.

At the conclusion of that event, my friend bought me a tape. (Remember them?) It was the *Andraé Crouch Live at Carnegie Hall* album. It's a classic.

What nobody knew was that I kept that tape in my car for the next two years. I would play it regularly when I was on my own. It moved me. I knew every song, and could quote almost every word spoken on that album. There were times when tears would flow. I was the only one who really knew what was happening in my heart.

Though I kept up a facade of spiritual indifference for the next three years, I knew that God was calling this wandering son home. Eventually I had no other option but to yield to that loving and persistent voice of the Father. I can testify that the fervent and faithful prayers of loving parents can change the direction of your life. My dad, Alex, experienced this when he had to trust God and wait (patiently) for me to hear the voice of God and turn aside from the lifestyle of my university days.

To you men who are on your knees interceding for your children: the prodigal's father gives great hope for the day you will run with open arms towards your son. My prayer for you is this: 'May the God of hope fill you with all joy and peace in believing, that you may abound in hope by the power of the Holy Spirit' (Romans 15:13 NKJV).

And to the sons: it's time to come home.

7. Chosen

Over the years, I've listened to the stories of men who have been adopted and who have experienced a gnawing ache to discover their biological parents. Some have had wonderful reunions while others have been disappointed. For some, the experience has led to a reopening of the father wound.

I have also met some incredible men who have stepped into the lives of broken families and become a father to the fatherless. These are the men who have become stepdads and adoptive parents. In doing so, they have played an important role in healing the father wound.

There is something very special about the adoption process. Parents expand their family, and they open their hearts and homes to welcome in a vulnerable child.

As one boy noted, when his siblings were teasing him because he was adopted, he confidently and humorously exclaimed, 'The difference between you and me is that I was chosen, but they were stuck with you.' He knew the joy of being chosen, and the wonder of being accepted (through adoption) into a family.

Possibly the most well-known stepdad in the Bible must be Joseph, the husband of Mary. He stepped up to take on the role of father to Mary's unborn child. In those times, the shame surrounding a woman carrying a child conceived out of wedlock was enormous. Yet Joseph stood by Mary, affirming her and accepting the child that he knew was not his.

It makes you realise that a father figure is so important to God that he would send his angel to speak to Joseph, with a commission to fill that earthly father void for his Son, Jesus, saying:

'Joseph son of David, do not be afraid to take Mary home as your wife, because what is conceived in her is from the Holy Spirit. She will give birth to a son, and you are to give him the name Jesus, because he will save his people from their sins.' (Matthew 1:20–21)

But there are many fatherless men who are not adopted into a new family. That's why God's promise of being a 'father to the fatherless' is so powerful and important. Take Psalm 68:5 as an example: 'A father to the fatherless, a defender of widows, is God in his holy dwelling.'

God's promise reaches its fruition in the life of Jesus. Through his death on the cross, we are reconciled to God and adopted into *his* family. We are not slaves or servants, but we are sons and daughters of the Father. And as such, we discover the wonder of unconditional love and unbridled acceptance. The Bible celebrates the fact that followers of Christ have been 'adopted' as sons. We've been accepted and chosen by him:

He predestined us for adoption to sonship through Jesus Christ, in accordance with his pleasure and will – to the praise of his glorious grace, which he has freely given us in the One he loves (Ephesians 1:5–6).

My friend Ken was adopted soon after he was born. He knew that from an early age. Though unsure what time in his life his adoptive parents had let him know, it never seemed to bother him growing up. His adoption has made it easier for him to understand that we are all 'adopted' into God's family.

Ken's story
'How I was conceived has not affected
who I have become.'

I knew I was different to the other siblings in my family. Even my outlook in life was very different to everyone else in the household. I'm forever grateful for the caring people who I call Mum and Dad though. They took me in, loved me, and treated me the same as everyone else.

There was never a moment in my life that I felt the need to meet my biological father. After I was conceived as the result of a short romance, that man walked out of my biological mother's life, not wanting to be either a husband or a dad.

When I was 23 years old, I met the woman who brought me into the world. It was by pure accident, as I had declined contact with her and other people connected to my biological family tree. On that first contact, she showed me photos of my biological father. I'm just not disappointed that I didn't meet that man. How I was conceived has not affected who I have become.

Being adopted has, in a special way, made it easy for me to understand God as a Father. In fact, being adopted into an earthly family has helped me accept that I have now been adopted into God's big family.

As a follower of Christ, I have discovered, through reading the Bible, that God genuinely wants to reveal himself as our Father. Furthermore, he has a very special place in his heart for those who feel abandoned:

> You, LORD, hear the desire of the afflicted;
> you encourage them, and you listen to their cry,
> defending the fatherless and the oppressed ...
> (Psalm 10:17–18)

Many adoptees, even with the most loving adoptive families, do wrestle with the pain of separation from their biological family, often with a sense of rejection and abandonment. But our heavenly Father knows we need to be anchored in unconditional love and acceptance.

So rest assured. If you do not have a biological father or have not found an adoptive earthly father, you have the Father whose love overcomes it all. You have a heavenly Father who will claim you, will adopt you, and will bring you home.

I vividly remember standing beside a woman as she spent time with the man who had adopted her over 60 years earlier – her father. He was in the final hours of this earthly life. Many words could have been said in that moment, but in their final exchange she used only five: 'Thank you for choosing me.'

What a magnificent understanding of the love and kindness that undergirded the acceptance she'd received. And when we're chosen by our heavenly Father, we can receive the same love, kindness and acceptance:

> The Spirit you received does not make you slaves, so that you live in fear again; rather, the Spirit you received brought about your adoption to sonship. And by him we cry, 'Abba, Father.' (Romans 8:15)

8. The Father's Call

God won't ever give up on you. He won't stop searching. He won't stop calling out to you, to bring you home.

I remember a time when our sons were young. We were in a busy shopping mall when one of them drifted away on his own. I thought my wife Lyn had him, and she thought I had him. It was holiday season. The crowds, the noise and the excitement caused him to go on an adventure and he became lost and alone. It's a horrible feeling when you realise that you have been separated from your son, and he is incredibly vulnerable.

I began to run through the centre calling his name. I cared little what people thought of me as I searched high and low for the son of mine who was lost. Those few minutes before we found him felt like hours.

Then there was the moment when he turned, having recognised my voice. He ran towards me, and I ran towards him. As I recall, it was just like on the movies – in slow motion. It was good to know that he was back, safe and in my arms.

Remember the story of the prodigal son that we talked about in chapter 6? The father running towards his son? That wonderful reunion? That's what your heavenly Father wants for you too. His ultimate desire is relationship with you.

There's a common misunderstanding about prayer that we need to address. It's not a monologue. Rather, like any conversation, it's meant to be two-way communication.

Let me explain.

Some of my most treasured memories are linked to heartfelt conversations I had with my dad, particularly in his latter years.

We would always start our conversations with a commentary on how our favourite sporting teams were performing. This was followed by a quick report on each of our extended family members. Then we would delve into the real issues – the matters of the heart. At times, we would laugh out loud. Other moments were quite tender and solemn.

One such occasion followed my request for an 'interview' in preparation for this book. He agreed, on the usual condition – that I arrived with a decent coffee and something 'nutritious' from the bakery. Caffeine and carbs were always his fuels of choice. So there we sat in the lounge room of his little unit with coffee and cake in hand. And we began to talk.

I realised sometime later that this conversation would be the last time he would ever open up to me about his childhood in such graphic detail. It was raw. It was real. It was rich! I am forever grateful that we both set time aside to talk like this. We both took the opportunity to speak, and to listen not only with our ears, but with our hearts.

Talking to God is the same. He wants to hear about your day … your life … everything.

But it also involves the discipline of listening. God wants to speak to you. If you are willing to dial back the busyness and the distractions of life, you will be amazed at how clearly the Lord is speaking to your heart.

Psalm 46:10 carries his invitation: 'Be still, and know that I am God.' You will hear your heavenly Father's voice most clearly when you take time out in a quiet place. In our modern lifestyle, that requires discipline. As you grow in relationship with him, you will learn to identify the ways in which God speaks to you. Here are a few.

The Bible. The Bible is full of such rich instruction. The Sermon on the Mount is full of such a wide range of subjects – teaching how to live a life of victory. Then there's the book of Proverbs, rich in wisdom. It's also hard to go past Paul's writings if you want to understand the person of Jesus, and who we can be with him in our lives.

Reading God's word is such a key to knowing him and hearing from him. There are promises in Scripture regarding the Holy Spirit helping us and guiding us in his truth. Someone once said that the Bible is the only book that promises that the author will turn up when we open it.

Preaching. There are lots of reasons why we should attend a good local church. God will often speak to our hearts when we sit under Bible-based teaching. A key thought. Fresh understanding. A challenge to respond. All of these can happen in those moments.

I once met a man at a conference who told me that something I had said, at a previous men's gathering, had so impacted him that he got the thought tattooed on his arm. While I found that a little extreme, I had to acknowledge that it obviously meant a lot to him. I must admit, though, that I prefer the easier option of writing those insights in a notebook.

Books and other resources. There is such good material available to us. We just have to access it.

Good friends. As I replay my life, it becomes apparent that God has spoken to me often when I've been in conversations with people who are a positive influence on my life. In those environments, when we start talking, he starts talking.

Impressions. These are those hard-to-define experiences. Even though we don't actually hear an audible voice, we know that we are given special understanding. It often feels like peace. Sometimes it's a warning. Some like to call it a premonition. But when we are walking in relationship with God, it's the Holy Spirit, gently speaking into our hearts.

On so many occasions that has happened to me. It's probably happened to you too. Perhaps you remember a moment in a church service or a Christian concert when you sensed the Father's call. It's not always easy to define, but you will recognise that undeniable 'still, small voice' of God drawing you closer to himself.

PART 3
The Father's Voice

Introduction

There is a gap in time between the Old and New Testaments in the Bible. The Old Testament ends with the following words in Malachi 4:6 (NKJV):

And he will turn
The hearts of the fathers to the children,
And the hearts of the children to their fathers,
Lest I come and strike the earth with a curse.

It's another four centuries before we have a record of God speaking again – in the New Testament. Imagine that – complete silence from heaven for 400 years.

You can only imagine the conversation among God's people, who wondered whether he would ever speak to them again: '*Will* he speak? *When* will he speak? And if he does – what will he say? Will he give us more rules, to add to the hundreds already in place under the law of the Old Testament? Will he chastise us for our wicked ways … or worse still, has he turned his back on humanity forever?' The silence continued.

It isn't until Jesus is baptised in the Jordan River that we hear again the voice of God. Then it happens! He speaks – at a significant moment in his Son's life: his baptism.

When all the people were being baptised, Jesus was baptised too. And as he was praying, heaven was opened and the Holy Spirit descended on him in bodily form like a dove. And a voice came from heaven: '*You are my Son, whom I love; with you I am well pleased*' (Luke 3:21–22).[1]

This is one of the rare times in Scripture when we see God the Father, God the Son and God the Holy Spirit – all three members of what we call the Trinity – at the same time, and in the same space. Something powerful, literally life-changing, is happening.

The Son, Jesus

The story begins with Jesus in the water, having just been baptised by John the Baptist. His baptism is a significant event that marks the start of his ministry, his work for his Father.

I'm not sure what your tradition is regarding baptism. My personal understanding and interpretation of the Scriptures sees baptism being an outward sign that testifies of an inward work of God in our life. It follows a decision to be a fully devoted follower of Christ. I will never forget the night I was baptised.

There's lots of great imagery associated with baptism by full immersion. It speaks of death and resurrection. Just as Jesus died and rose again, so too have I died to my old ways, and I'm now living in his resurrection power, having given him Lordship over my life.

This act of baptism has really helped a lot of people in their spiritual journey. I know it helped me.

We need to be clear, though: there's nothing magic in the water; but there is something powerful in obeying the leading of the Lord in our life. If you are a follower of Christ, and this is something that resonates with you, perhaps now is a good time to discuss water baptism with a trusted Christian leader.

If your tradition or doctrine places baptism differently, then let's not argue on this point. We do know that Jesus was in the water being baptised, and it's in that place where a big lesson lies.

The Holy Spirit

After Jesus was baptised, the Holy Spirit appeared from above in 'bodily form like a dove' and descended upon him. From then on, Jesus and the Holy Spirit were inseparable companions.

Jesus needed the Holy Spirit to fulfil his mission. In the Bible, we read of 'how God anointed Jesus of Nazareth with the Holy Spirit and power, and how he went around doing good and healing all who were under the power of the devil, because God was with him' (Acts 10:38).

The Father

Then, the third member of the Trinity spoke – the Father in heaven. Imagine what the voice of God would sound like. (Lots of reverb on the sound system is my initial thought.) In Psalm 29, the psalmist David describes it as a voice that 'thunders over the mighty waters' (v. 3), breaking cedar trees, twisting oak trees and shaking the desert (vv. 5, 8–9).

Yet it was different this time. God spoke directly to his Son. He affirmed Jesus, standing there in the river, as his Son. In the process, he expressed three things every son needs to hear from his father:

- You are my son.
- I love you.
- I'm proud of you.

Deep down, everyone knows what they should receive from their father. When it's missing, there's that wound, the 'father void', in a person's life. No-one and nothing appears to be able to fill it.

We've been told to never go shopping when we are hungry. If we do, there is the possibility that we will buy junk food – items filled with sugar that we rapidly consume. The sugar hit gives us a rush, but we come off that quickly. We need something more substantial that will sustain us and satisfy our hunger. The hungry souls of humanity without God often seek to fill the emptiness in our hearts in all the wrong places. Filling up on the junk food of the soul, we are left feeling unsatisfied.

God knew that without a relationship with him, there was something missing in the human race – a problem that had to be addressed. When God broke his silence, he didn't proclaim his power or declare his judgement. God the Father affirmed his Son, and the message of love is true for all of us:

You are my son.

I love you.

I'm proud of you.

Let's take a closer look at those three life-changing affirmations so you can hear them too.

9. Identity: 'You Are My Son ...'

Have you ever played the kids' game 'Who am I?' It's fairly simple. A name card is placed on the head of each participant. The participants then take turns at trying to identify who they are by asking questions. Usually with enough hints and enough time, they can work out who their character is. There are, though, those who just can't work out who they are.

That's okay when we're playing games, but not in real life. Sadly, some people, well into adulthood, still haven't worked out the answer to one of life's big questions: Who am I?

Some of you might have watched the *Bourne* movie series – action-thrillers centred on the character Jason Bourne. How good are these movies?! In a (very) brief summary of the plot, a government operative has been reprogrammed and his name changed. He's been told he's Jason Bourne, but he's not. The energy in the plot is driven by a man who needs to know who he really is. After a long journey hunting down his real identity, he eventually discovers who he actually is: a completely different person named David Webb. It is only then that he can stop searching and rest.

It's a classic example of how imperative it is that we discover who we really are. Having the wrong identity creates a tension within us.

I'm sure you've been to one of those parties where you are encouraged to dress according to a certain theme. Seriously, I don't get excited about those things, but a few years ago my sister had one of those milestone birthdays, and she requested that everybody who attended dressed in 1950s style. I obliged. It was actually a lot of fun.

The main entertainment for the night was an Elvis Presley impersonator. He started well. He talked like Elvis. He dressed like Elvis. He walked like Elvis. And most importantly, he sang like Elvis ... well, sort of.

As the evening wore on, it became apparent that he was enjoying this a lot more than anyone else in the room. It was a little awkward. I quietly shuffled to the back of the room and whispered to a friend, 'He walks like Elvis. He talks like Elvis. He dresses like Elvis. But I think he's the only one in the room unaware of one important fact. He's *not* Elvis!'

Plenty of people in our world are working really hard to be somebody else, rather than being comfortable with who they are. They're impersonators pretending to be somebody else, and pretending is pretty tiring. Eventually, we have to face that internal question: 'Who am I?'

Some men try to find identity in what they do: their work. And we do tend to label people by their job or career – describing people as 'Fred the plumber' or 'John the accountant'. Sometimes we add an adjective, like 'successful'. Somehow that's meant to convey a message or form an image, even impress other people. But when we find our entire identity in our career, we are headed for disappointment. We are not human *doings*. We are human *beings*.

Other people find their identity in what they own: their property and possessions. I met a man when speaking at a business conference a number of years ago. As we walked together, I admired his expensive sports car. When I mentioned that I could never afford a vehicle like it, he told me how much it had cost him – three marriages! Sometimes the price for things we think we need, for our image or our sense of self-worth, is just too high.

Then there are those who try to find their core identity in relationships. How many people do you know who've tried to find their self-worth in the number of high-profile connections they can boast about or their sexual conquests? Or their number of 'likes' on Facebook as people turn to social media to find their self-worth and identity? And, ironically, people may have hundreds of Facebook friends but no-one to talk to.

I have to admit, I've been greatly entertained over the years by *The Simpsons*. Before you judge me, I want you to know that an English literature academic was interviewed while visiting our nation once. He was an expert in the works of Shakespeare. When asked whether anything in contemporary art matched Shakespeare for satire and social commentary, he replied, 'I can only think of one thing: *The Simpsons*.' I felt affirmed.

In one very special episode, Lisa, the overachiever in the family, discovers that her substitute teacher Mr Bergstrom is leaving her school for another assignment. She's shattered and begs him to stay. After declaring her deep love and gratitude to this man whom she calls her favourite teacher, it becomes obvious that he is moving on.

Picture the scene. They are at a train station, and Mr Bergstrom is preparing to board his train. Before he leaves, he says, 'When you're alone and have no-one to rely on, this is all you need to know,' and he proceeds to write a note on a piece of paper. He folds it and hands it to Lisa.

As the train pulls away from the station, Lisa runs beside it. Just before the train takes him away, out of sight and out of her life forever, Mr Bergstrom opens the window of his carriage and farewells Lisa, yelling, 'It will be okay … just read the note.'

So she stops. She reads it. There are just four words on that note: 'You are Lisa Simpson.'

Into our world, for only a short time, came a wonderful teacher – Jesus Christ. He taught us profound things – truths we'd never heard before. We hoped he would stay around forever. However, it was obvious that he planned to leave for another place. Thankfully, he's left us a note. It's called the Bible, and it clearly tells us who we are and what we can be.

Here's an encouraging note. The words are about the teacher himself, found in John 1:12: 'to all who did receive him, to those who believed in his name, he gave the right to become the children of God.' The basis for Jesus' identity was in his relationship with God the Father.

Let me say that again: the basis for Jesus' identity was in his relationship with God the Father.

He did not need external factors to bolster his self-worth. Not titles. Not possessions or position. Even in the face of intense criticism, he was unshakable because he knew who he was. He'd heard his Father say, 'You are my Son, whom I love; with you I am well pleased' (Luke 3:22).

That's all he needed. That's all any one of us needs.

While Jesus knew who he was, it took a bit longer for his first followers to realise. In Matthew 16, Jesus asked them if people knew who he was. In response to his question, they replied: 'Some say John the Baptist; others say Elijah; and still others, Jeremiah or one of the prophets' (v. 14).

Then came the most important question of them all: 'But what about you?' he asked. 'Who do you say I am?' (v. 15).

If you've read anything in the Gospels, you won't be surprised to know that Simon Peter happily spoke for the group, answering, 'You are the Messiah, the Son of the living God' (v. 16).

Jesus replied, 'Blessed are you, Simon son of Jonah, for this was not revealed to you by flesh and blood, but by my Father in heaven' (v. 17).

There's something wonderful that happens when I discover who Jesus is. He helps me discover who I am. That's what he did for Simon that day: 'And I tell you that you are Peter, and on this rock I will build my church, and the gates of Hades will not overcome it' (v. 18).

Once Peter (whose name means 'rock') had a clear understanding of Jesus' identity, Jesus gave him his identity and something else: an invitation to embark on life's great adventure – showing the love of the Father to a lost and hurting world.

That is why Jesus taught us to address God as 'our Father' when we pray. When I call him 'Father', it not only helps me identify who he is, but it also clarifies who I am – his son!

10. Value: '... Whom I Love ...'

Ernest Hemingway, in his short story 'The Capital of the World', tells the story of Paco, a young man in Spain who runs away from home. His father hopes he will return quickly, but that doesn't happen. Another 'prodigal son'. The shame, guilt and regret he feels prevents Paco from returning home to his father. Paco doesn't know that his father has been searching for him ever since he left.

One day, Paco's father puts an advertisement in the local newspaper of Madrid, *El Liberal*. It reads: 'Paco, meet me at the Hotel Montana at noon on Tuesday. All is forgiven! Love Papa.' But Paco is a common name in Spain; and when the father approaches the planned meeting place, he finds 800 young men there all named Paco, all waiting for their fathers, all hoping for forgiveness.

Everyone needs to know that they are forgiven – that they are loved. We men may present a tough exterior, but we long to hear the words of our father saying, 'I love you, son.' You are never too young and never too old to hear it.

That was reinforced by a phone call I took one Saturday morning from a friend who is in his 60s. After a short conversation about common interests, we began to discuss the contents of this book. I told him, 'Every son needs to hear their dad say they love them.'

Things went quiet on the other end. He finally said, with some emotion, 'I agree. My dad just can't do it. He never has.'

How sad. What makes it even sadder is that his father is well known for helping other people in a professional capacity.

The same word can mean different things to different people. As you travel internationally, you discover that words that are spelled the same, even pronounced the same, don't always mean the same. If you go to South Africa, for example, people may refer to a 'robot'. The first time I heard that, I was looking for something akin to R2D2. The locals knew what it meant, but I didn't: a robot in that country is a set of traffic lights.

Likewise, a dairy in New Zealand is a corner store. Go figure! Same word. Different meaning. And let's not tell our friends in the USA that we wear thongs on our feet.

The same applies to the word 'love'. In many cases, it seems that we have lost the depth of the meaning of the word. Perhaps it's through overuse? We hear men say 'I love my truck. I love my football team. I really love meat pies … Oh, and I love you too.' That really puts the special people in our lives among some auspicious company. (I think not!)

So what does 'love' really mean when we talk about God's love? One of the best descriptions of the Father's – and Jesus' – love, and the love we are to show others, is found in 1 Corinthians 13:4–8:

> Love is patient, love is kind. It does not envy, it does not boast, it is not proud. It does not dishonour others, it is not self-seeking, it is not easily angered, it keeps no record of wrongs. Love does not delight in evil but rejoices with the truth. It always protects, always trusts, always hopes, always perseveres. Love never fails …

Read those last three words again. One of the most important and defining characteristics of the love of the Father is that it *never* fails. It is extravagant and it is unconditional. Nothing we can do can make him love us more. Nothing we can do can make him love us less. He loves us ... full stop.

In other words, I'm not loved because I'm valuable; I'm valuable because I'm loved. Jesus knew that as God's Son, and we can too. We simply need to comprehend how much we are loved.

If you ever doubt your worth to God, look to the cross. Here you will see the most powerful demonstration of love that humanity has ever witnessed: 'But God demonstrates his own love for us in this: while we were still sinners, Christ died for us' (Romans 5:8).

Take that in. Make it personal. Christ died for *you*. Was there ever such a powerful expression of the Father's love?

In the world of athletics, the 400 metre sprint event is demanding. At the 1992 Barcelona Olympics, British sprinter Derek Redmond had done very well in the heats. Leading into the semifinal, there were high expectations that he could win a medal.

He went to the starting blocks and waited. The gun went off. He got a good start. Then it happened. At the halfway mark, Redmond suffered a bad tear to his hamstring, causing him to immediately drop to the ground. He was shattered. Four years of hard work – the training and the sacrifice – all seemed lost, as the other runners passed him on their way to the finish line.

Rather than receive medical assistance, he got back up and hobbled around the track, obviously in great pain but determined to complete the final 200 metres. When the crowd noticed what was happening they began to cheer. But the drama was far from finished.

At the last 100 metre mark, someone climbed over the fence, pushed past the officials and joined Derek on the final run towards the finish line. It was his dad, Jim. If you ever watch a replay of this event, you will see Olympic officials trying to stop Jim from helping his son, but he pushes them away every time. He appears to be yelling at them, too. It looks something like 'Go away; I'm his dad!'

When the two of them crossed the finish line, a roar equal to that given to the winner went up for the young man who completed his task, which was only possible because of the support of his father. Again, love in action.

A lot of fathers, though, aren't like Jim. Many struggle to express their love, through words or actions, to their sons and daughters, or to articulate their affection. It is hard to love when you haven't been loved.

Let's go back to that moment in the Jordan River when Jesus is baptised. As he comes out of the water, he hears his Father say 'I love you.' Something powerful transpires when we declare to someone 'I love you'. Jesus heard it from his Father, and he was secure in the knowledge of the unconditional love the Father had for him. Living in the knowledge of that love meant that he never needed to look for his value in anyone or anything else. What else matters when you know how deeply you are loved by the Creator of the universe?

Such pure love is much more than a feeling. It transcends sentiment. It's enriching. And importantly, once you have received it, you'll find it easy to pass it on. When we come to understand how much we are loved by God, it becomes easier to give love to others. Once my father discovered his heavenly Father's love, he was able to express his love to me, his son. The love of God stopped the generational paralysis.

'You are my Son ... and I love you.' Jesus received his Father's love, so he could freely give it. He modelled this love throughout his life, and the Bible overflows with examples of Jesus' love in action – a love that knows no boundaries.

He healed lepers, disregarding cultural norms that considered lepers to be unclean and untouchable (Matthew 8:1–4). He spent time talking to a Samaritan woman, who belonged to a group of people who were religious outcasts (John 4:4–26). He befriended a tax collector named Zacchaeus, who was ostracised in his culture because he worked with the occupying forces, the Romans (Luke 19:1–10).

And Jesus' ultimate expression of love in action was his death on the cross, for us – for you.

'You are my son, whom I love.'

Love is a powerful force. It *never* fails.

11. Confidence: '… With You I Am Well Pleased'

I would like to take some credit for my sons' athletic achievements. Along with the obligations of transport to training and paying for the necessary equipment, my major contribution was being their number one cheerleader.

Though athletics was not the primary sport in our home, the boys competed in various school athletics carnivals. I was particularly excited to find that my schedule allowed me to be present at one of their cross-country races.

Mingling with a number of other parents waiting for their sons to emerge from the nearby bushland that made up a portion of the track, I noticed that my son was in second place and closing in on the leader. As they approached the final hundred metres, they ran past me and excitement got the better of me. I began to run beside my son, cheering him on. 'Go son. Run harder. You can do this,' I shouted. To which my champion offspring, somewhat exhausted, turned and replied, 'Oh Dad. Shut up.'

I may have stopped running beside my sons, but I've never stopped cheering them on. Because that is what a good father does.

I don't watch a lot of reality shows, but the few that I've seen tend to have a common theme: contestants are expected to survive the toughest of situations. In the course of a show, we often discover that they are motivated by a need to prove themselves to others, especially those they admire. It's common to find that that person is their father.

An older man from our church told me once, 'I don't know what my father thought of me. He never told me … and he died before I had the opportunity to ask him.'

The 'performance trap' is something that most men are vulnerable to. Our ego calls us to impress others for our own benefit. There's a term that is not terribly complimentary: a 'try-hard'. It refers to somebody who goes to extreme lengths, over-performing in certain areas, in order to lift people's view of them. Often it's a case of them really wanting to feel better about themselves, and it's usually a reflection of their own internal battle.

Jesus was immune from the performance trap, despite many opportunities to flaunt his power. One opportunity arose just before the start of his public ministry, and it is recorded in Luke 4:1–13. Here, in the wilderness, he was tempted by Satan three times.

First, Satan encouraged Jesus to turn stone into bread. Although Jesus had been fasting for 40 days, he resisted, refusing to display his power for Satan.

Second, Satan appealed to Jesus' ego, taking him to a place where he could see 'all the kingdoms of the world' and saying:

'I will give you all their authority and splendour; it has been given to me, and I can give it to anyone I want to. If you worship me, it will all be yours' (vv. 5–7).

Jesus' response is a great example of why it's important to read the Bible and memorise Scripture. You have it to guide you when times get tough. Jesus countered this temptation by saying, 'It is written: "Worship the Lord your God and serve him only"' (v. 8).

Third, Satan dared Jesus to display his divinity:

> The devil led him to Jerusalem and had him stand on the highest point of the temple. 'If you are the Son of God,' he said, 'throw yourself down from here' (v. 9).

There was a subtlety in this temptation. It challenged the Son's identity: '*If* you are the Son of God ...'. That gained no traction, because Jesus was secure and confident in the knowledge of who he was.

Jesus is the holy Son of God, but he was also a man with unimaginable power at his command. Yet he refused to do anything that Satan asked him to do; he did not need to perform to prove himself. Throughout Jesus' earthly ministry, he modelled confidence, security and strength. The reason? He'd heard his Father say, 'With you I am well pleased' – or, using our language, 'I'm proud of you, son.'

It really doesn't matter who you are or how old you are; there is something incredible that happens in the soul of a man when he hears his dad say, 'I'm proud of you.'

My father often attended church services where I was preaching. If you've ever preached, or spoken publicly, you will be aware that there are days when everything you say just seems to flow so smoothly. They're good days! And then there are the other days. I've had a couple of them ... okay, quite a few.

They were the times that I would look out into the crowd, past the faces of those whose eyes had glazed over, and I would find an old man who was there to worship God, and if needed, encourage his son. I never heard him yell out in a service, but he would give me a simple 'thumbs up' when I caught his eye.

Sometimes no words are necessary. We had an understanding. I knew what he was saying: 'Keep going, and never forget that I'm proud of you, son.'

The joy that God the Father had in his Son was also expressed later in Jesus' ministry on earth, on the Mount of Transfiguration. By now Jesus was a public figure, enjoying what most would call success and prominence. But it was still only the affirmation of the Father that mattered:

> While he was still speaking, a bright cloud covered them, and a voice from the cloud said, 'This is my Son, whom I love; with him I am well pleased. Listen to him!' (Matthew 17:5).

Jesus knew who he was and *whose* he was. When he faced the greatest challenge of all, an excruciating and humiliating death on a cross for the sins of the world, he could do it in the full assurance of his Father's love and affirmation.

Fathers have an incredible responsibility: to build confidence in their children through encouragement. Each one is unique and possesses attributes that we need to celebrate.

King David understood how unique he was: 'I praise you because I am fearfully and wonderfully made; your works are wonderful, I know that full well' (Psalm 139:14). He knew that everything about him was personalised.

Every human being who's ever been born has features specific to them personally. Our fingerprint is one example. The surfaces of our eyes and tongues are not shared with anyone else either. No-one is a carbon copy of another. We are all one-off masterpieces who deserve to be celebrated. Who better to celebrate our skills, efforts and personhood than our dads? That's one of my most significant commitments in life. I trust it's yours too.

I'm grateful for parents who helped finance my tertiary education while knowing my destiny was to be a preacher. I had that lofty dream of being a marine biologist, but then reality kicked in. It was obvious that the course I was doing would leave me with a Bachelor of Applied Unemployment. My revised studies were really enjoyable and gave me a great career path. All through those years, I was encouraged and loved. I was never pushed to follow in my father's footsteps.

I learned an important lesson, looking back on that season. Real faith is open-handed. It does not try to manipulate situations, and gives up on trying to control outcomes. As parents, one of the most encouraging things we can do for our kids is to let them discover who they really are for themselves, and trust God to guide them into their future. They will be empowered, and in the process, greatly encouraged.

Not everyone reading this book excelled in the subject of English at school, so indulge me as I draw from my extensive learnings in Year 6 English. There are things called prefixes. They are two or three letters attached to the start of a word which completely change the meaning of that word.

For example, 'courage', which means strength in the face of a battle, is changed when we add the letters 'en' at the front. It becomes 'encourage'; and 'en', my English teacher told me, means 'to put into'. So when I encourage someone, I put strength for the fight into them. I've watched a lot of young men walk a little taller and believe they can embrace a significant challenge on the back of a few kind words. They've been encouraged.

Dwight L Moody was instrumental in establishing the YMCA. He was a noted preacher whose influence extended way beyond his generation. He had a motto: 'People don't become what you nag them into. They become what you encourage them to be.' Great dads know this.

Is this a good time to put this book down and take a minute to tell one of your children that you are proud of them?

12. Hearing His Voice

My life has been framed by things God has spoken into my heart. When I was nine years old, I remember telling my parents, 'I was called to be a preacher today.' They seemed pleased, but were disappointingly low-key in their response to my news. They told me many years later that they had known that call on my life ever since I was a baby. My declaration was not a surprise to them. God had been speaking with them, too.

In chapter 6, I shared with you a part of my own story, where I went off on my own, doing my own thing. Here is the part where God called me back, speaking to me through other Christian men.

Not long after my twentieth birthday, three men came into my life in three consecutive weeks, each of them believing they had a message for me straight from the heart of God. Incredibly, it was the same message repeated three times. God was wanting to get my attention, so he positioned people in my life to speak on his behalf.

I remained quite stoic on the first two occasions, but by the third time I gave up. I chose to follow Jesus … and I've done so ever since.

In that early phase of following Jesus, I still had a lot to learn about how to follow God and do things his way. My biggest personal challenge in those days as a Christian was to totally surrender to the Lord and place him first in every area of my life.

There was one important moment in that season that was quite poignant. A friend of mine was a broker in quality water ski boats. He called me one day to say that he had the very thing I'd been looking for – a magnificent ski race boat, fully equipped with a massive 454 cubic inch inboard motor. It was amazing. Its stunning looks were only surpassed by the incredible noise it made. After a few minutes of warming up the engine, the time came to let the 'beast' loose. I lost no time in opening up the throttle and we sped across the water. It was exhilarating until something hit me in the eye and I lost control of the boat.

I hadn't worn the protective eyewear needed for high-speed boating, so a huge bug had flown into my eye! It hit me with such force that I loosened my grip on the wheel and the boat swerved dangerously. It could have been all over as I struggled to regain control of the boat at speed. Thankfully I did, and we returned, at a much slower speed, to the boat ramp.

Not long after that, I was back in my car driving home. That's when I heard that voice again. It was my heavenly Father, calling me to decide who and what would be master of my life. The next day, I cancelled the purchase of the boat. It was a defining 'follow me' moment.

There have been other significant moments over the years when I have seen (in a vision) a roadmap for my life unfolding. And there have been different phases – including helping young people, stepping into new roles of Christian leadership, and serving others in various capacities – when I've been certain that God has spoken to me and shown me a pathway to a fulfilling life. Through it all, I've discovered that when God calls, he has something good in store for me.

My personal journey has definitely been fuelled by those who encouraged me along the way. They're the people who saw more potential in me than I saw in myself. Ultimately, however, the defining force that undergirds my life, transcending all other factors, is the knowledge that I've heard the voice of my Father.

Just as God spoke to Jesus, he speaks to all his children. And what he spoke over Jesus, he speaks over you: 'You are mine and I love you.'

I'm not sure I've ever heard God's audible voice, but I do know when he's 'speaking' to me. It's possible that you have 'heard' him too. It could have happened when you've read the Bible, while you've been sitting in a church, or while you've been quietly enjoying the beauty of creation. It could be a word in your mind, a phrase, a recurring thought, a picture or a vision. It's hard to describe, but when it happens, you know it's real. And though it's rarely audible, it's always affirming. Though he may challenge us about areas in our life, he will never condemn us. He speaks. He calls, always desiring to draw us close. If you have given your life to Jesus, you will 'hear' the Father's love too, claiming you, affirming you, and loving you as his precious child.

'You are my Son, whom I love; with you I am well pleased' (Luke 3:22). He gives identity, value and confidence.

PART 4

The Journey

Introduction

God will take you the way you are, but he won't leave you the way you are. He leads us on a journey that will heal our hearts and help us heal others. Forgiveness is our Father's signature move. It's the first step he takes with us as we walk with him.

On a beautiful sunny Brisbane morning, I sat chatting with my dad over a cup of tea. I listened as he told me about what happened after he gave his life to Jesus.

After I kneeled in the gutter to give my life to Jesus, I began a journey, walking with the Lord, that continued for the next seventy years.

Few thought my decision would last. After all, I was drunk at the time. My life was a mess, and it showed. When I was saved, I was the talk of the town, but there were a number of speed bumps on the way.

A short time later, I went to work for a pest exterminator in Barcaldine in outback Queensland. This is where the Holy Spirit spoke to me about going to Bible college.

The very thought of it frightened the daylights out of me. So, like Jonah, I ran away from that thought. Then one day I was a walking past a hotel. I felt tempted to go in and have a beer. My instant reply was, 'You know I don't drink!' Then I sensed the Holy Spirit say, 'Well, you may as well because you won't do as you're told.' I caught the very next train to Brisbane where the college was!'

Attending Bible college was a big challenge. I was a country boy at heart and hardly knew anything about theology or the

Scriptures. Mixing with all those people who already knew the Bible backwards was intimidating. I didn't even know where the book of Revelation was. 'What have I let myself into?' I wondered.

Even though Alex felt out of his depth, he persevered. That first step of going to Bible college may have been hard, but it set him on a journey that changed not only him, but the Alcorn family and many others. It was, however, one step at a time.

Overcoming the pain of abandonment or abuse or dealing with unresolved conflicts, particularly with our fathers, is never a single event. It is a journey. And let's face it: while some journeys may be short, most take considerable time.

The Holy Spirit will guide you and teach you all things – that's a promise from your Father: 'But the Advocate, the Holy Spirit, whom the Father will send in my name, will teach you all things and will remind you of everything I have said to you' (John 14:26).

Let's look at how, guided by the Holy Spirit, you can take steps on your journey with the Lord.

13. Where Are You Now?

The first steps on any journey – particularly a journey of faith – will often take a lot of courage. As Alex discovered, the starting point usually involves honesty, humility and submission to his Lordship in our life.

In chapter 1 we heard Sam's story – a raw and honest account of how his father left the family when Sam was a teenager. Years later, he had to confront his pain.

Sam's story (continued)
'What the heck was that?'

I was sitting in the front row of church, watching a singer at a Christmas event. One of the songs was about a little girl whose dad had left the family.

It describes how the father needs to take a second job to pay alimony and maintenance for the family, so he finds work as a Santa in a shopping centre. One day, he sees his 9-year-old daughter in the line. He panics, but realises he is disguised by his Santa suit, so he masks his voice with a cheery 'Ho, ho, ho' as the little girl sits on his knee. The little girl tells Santa that all she wants is for her father to be home for Christmas.

I was sitting there, a 23-year-old married man, and this unresolved pain from my past struck me. My shoulders shuddered with emotion, and I was inconsolable. It was embarrassing to become undone in public.

When I got home that night, I thought, 'What the heck was that?'

I felt the Holy Spirit say, 'I've been trying to do that for a while.'

Another phase of healing had begun in my life.

If you're going to take a journey, there are some important questions to ask yourself before you begin:

- Where are you now?
- Where do you want to go?
- How are you going to get there?
- Are you carrying any excess baggage?

We will unpack these questions here and in the coming chapters.

It's always a fun time when your children get their licences and begin to drive their own cars. I remember one of my boys phoning me one day to ask me how to get to a certain location. He'd driven a considerable distance and was concerned that he was off course. Before I could answer his question, I had to ask him, 'Where are you at the moment? Give me some reference points.' Once we identified his current location, I was able to send him on his journey to his preferred destination.

In the Bible, the first question asked by God is in Genesis 3:9. God asked Adam, 'Where are you?' Do you really think that God had lost Adam – that he was concerned that he had only made one human and now he'd lost him? Of course not! God was actually giving Adam an opportunity to be found. Simply put, Adam had to admit where he was so that God could begin to help him.

There are some magnificent therapeutic programs available to assist us on our journey these days. None of them, however, is of assistance unless we acknowledge the reality of our current situation. Some of us have started wrestling with issues, while others have been denying important incidents in our past. But this is the time.

It's your time to go on a journey and walk out the healing your soul desperately needs. This is incredibly important for you personally. It's also imperative that you find the freedom that's available to you, so that the generations that follow you will benefit too.

Whenever you turn on the GPS in your vehicle, it identifies your starting position. Never have I had that nameless 'lady' that lives inside that device ever react to my starting position. She's never come back with disappointment in her voice and said, 'Don't tell me that you are *there!*' No. We need to know exactly where we are before we can head to where we would prefer to be.

And just as my GPS is never concerned with my starting position, neither is God. In God's kingdom, honesty is always the best policy. That's why King David prayed: 'Search me, God, and know my heart; test me and know my anxious thoughts' (Psalm 139:23). He was simply wanting to acknowledge before God where things were in his life.

It's useless to pretend that God doesn't know. He just needs us to admit our current location in order for the exciting journey to begin.

So where are you at … honestly?

Be authentic in your assessment of the important things in your life: marriage, family, faith, health, financial freedom.

Are you struggling with things that you hope nobody ever discovers? Justifying your lack of attention to dealing with matters like these will get you nowhere.

But I have good news. You don't have to stay where you are. It's never too late to become the man you could be, but you will need to face the facts about your current 'location'. It's time to have a blunt conversation with the man in the mirror. Denial won't help, but honesty will.

It may come as a surprise for you to know that there are men in your world who are waiting to walk with you once you acknowledge your willingness to take the first step. You just have to be honest about where you're currently at.

14. Where Do You Want to Go?

If you don't know where you want to go, it won't matter what path you take. 'Whatever' will be one of your favourite words. Discipline, diligence and commitment will be absent from your lifestyle. You will just go with the flow. The biggest problem with this is that you can't guarantee that *the flow* will take you to a great place.

Solomon reminds us that 'Where there is no revelation, people cast off restraint' (Proverbs 29:18). The word 'revelation' can also be translated as 'dream' or 'vision'. If you don't have a clear view of a great future, you won't care what road you take in life.

I've had men tell me that they don't have a vision for their life. I simply ask them, 'What would you like to do? What would you like to become?' Vision and desire are usually the same thing. 'Take delight in the LORD, and he will give you the desires of your heart' (Psalm 37:4).

For now, try to identify where you would like some of those key areas of your life to be in one year, three years, even ten years from now. It's worth writing those things down. *That's* your preferred destination.

There is a prophet in the Bible named Habakkuk. His writings are found in a short book towards the end of the Old Testament. Most of the book is filled with complaints about situations all around him, yet there's a shift in the tone as chapter 2 begins.

He makes a profound comment that can be easily missed but is filled with great understanding:

> I will stand at my watch
> and station myself on the ramparts;
> I will look to see what he will say to me,
> and what answer I am to give to this complaint.
> (Habakkuk 2:1)

'I will look to see what he will say to me.' Such insight! This man of God recognised that when God speaks to us – when he puts something in our hearts – it can be so clear that we can almost see it. God-given dreams and desires can have the same affect.

Some men need to give themselves permission to dream again – to see the possibilities of the future, despite some of the setbacks of their past. A wise man once said, 'The poorest man in the world is not the man without the money. It's the man without the dream.'

Can you give yourself permission to dream of better days ahead? Can you dare to imagine a life beyond what you've known – living above the humdrum of mediocrity? More importantly, can you see yourself free of the 'inevitability trap' that's held generations of men in your family line captive?

If you can, statements like 'Our family has always been this way' will not fit in your vocabulary anymore. A bold and exciting dream will get you up every morning, well before the alarm clock.

Life's journey brings us to a number of T-intersections. They are the points where we have major choices to make. That's when you need more than a dream. You need a strategy.

15. How Are You Going to Get There?

I'm sure we've all got horror stories about road trips that didn't go according to plan. We may hate to admit it, but there is a real possibility that our failure to plan may be the cause. (Let's not talk about men's aversion to asking for directions!)

You need a strategy: a roadmap that will take the big idea of your preferred destination and break it down into small sections. It's in the strategy that you can measure incremental improvements.

Let me warn you: you can expect to hear negative voices along your journey. Fatigue will tell you that it's too hard. Disappointment will tell you that no-one cares whether you make it. Sentiment will try to lure you back to the 'good old days'. Without a robust strategy, you are at risk of taking sidetracks, or worse still, turning around and going back to where you once were.

Later, we will look at the benefits of having a mentor in your life. This is the kind of person who can be very helpful to you in developing your plans. They will also play an important part in holding you accountable to your roadmap.

The principles of the Bible are a tremendous asset to help us navigate the complexities of life's journey. Of the various descriptions that the Bible ascribes to itself, one of the clearest comes from Psalms: 'Your word is a lamp for my feet, a light on my path' (Psalm 119:105).

A lamp for my feet helps me identify where I'm standing right now. A light on my path helps me look ahead to a brighter future. I know no better compass than God's word. Reading it daily brings strength to our life, and clarity to our journey.

Continual assessment

Every journey also requires continual assessment. Am I on the right track? How am I doing?

There are a few questions that we should ask ourselves on a regular basis, no matter whether life has treated us well or our past has been really rough. Try these for starters:

- *My identity*: Is it becoming less defined by others' opinions and more defined by personal awareness? Am I willing to be vulnerable with safe people in my world – happy to let them see the real me rather than a facade?

- *My value*: Knowing that I am loved by God, am I able to express love more freely to others now? How am I demonstrating that?

- *My confidence*: Does insecurity have less of a grip on my life than it used to? In what ways is that evident?

Some men have found journalling to be helpful to gauge their progress in life. It's a great way to reflect on God's word and apply the challenges it brings to your heart, too.

Fuel for the journey

We can't ignore the fact that we will need fuel for a journey. The dashboard of my car has a gauge that informs me of the amount of fuel I have remaining in my tank, and with that an estimate of how far that fuel will get me.

It can be stressful when you're not sure you are going to complete your trip, especially if you are alone. It's just wise to keep a sufficient amount of fuel in your tank. This is where setting margins in your life is so important, instead of burning yourself out. Do you know what 'fills your tank'?

There are actually three tanks: your physical, emotional and spiritual tanks.

Physical

Guys aren't always good at taking care of themselves. But if we are going to last the journey, we had better take personal responsibility for things like exercise, diet and rest.

Have you had a physical check-up lately? I know the thought of the snap of the doctor's rubber glove brings chills to any man. Let me assure you: you will be fine. It really is a good idea to keep your eye on the basic health gauges.

Emotional

What makes you feel fully alive? I know what it is for me:

- The ocean: being out there at sunrise is good for the soul. Landing a decent fish at the same time is an added bonus.

- The bush: hiking on a mountain, or just walking in God's creation resets me.

- Sport: anywhere a sweaty man is chasing a ball catches my interest, especially if he is wearing Maroon, or Green and Gold. I do have mental images of me still being an incredible sportsperson. Though that might not be a true reflection of reality, I still enjoy getting out there and having fun.

What about you? Where do you find wonder? How regularly do you allocate time to engage with it?

Spiritual

A regular time of personal devotion provides us with an amazing start to our day. Encounters with the Divine enable us to tackle the issues and obstacles we'll face.

Let me suggest a wonderful ingredient to include in your spiritual tank: gratitude. We can be thankful daily for God's goodness – his love and mercy. There are also the things that we sometimes take for granted but are precious. Our health, friends, every new day … life itself! People who aren't grateful have a dullness about their spirit.

No wonder the Bible encourages us to be thankful when we come to God. Here's the way *The Message*'s translation of a well-known Scripture puts it:

> Enter with the password: 'Thank you!'
> Make yourselves at home, talking praise.
> Thank him. Worship him (Psalm 100:4).[1]

Something that impresses me about every GPS unit I've ever seen is that they are never overwhelmed by the length of the journey. Nor do they overload the traveller with too much information. They simply give the next step. That's all that's important – the next step.

So what's your next step to improving those important areas of your life? Marriage. Family. Other relationships. Health. Finances. There is no better day than today to start that journey with a simple step forward.

16. Are You Carrying Any Excess Baggage?

Some people you meet leave an indelible mark on your memory. This was the case with one young man I encountered one Sunday morning after speaking at a local church. He told me something very special had happened the night before. The authorities had finally taken the electronic monitoring device off his ankle. It obviously meant a lot to him. He'd been in prison and his hard life was evident on his exterior.

A mature-aged couple standing nearby were beaming with delight, ever so proud of him. I was told they had visited him regularly right through his time in prison and had 'adopted' him as a son.

His news was particularly special because he'd recently made a genuine decision to be a Christ-follower. Everything about his life had taken a wonderful turn for good. At the end of the conversation the three of them left, walking, hugging and celebrating in one happy motion.

Afterwards, the pastor of the church told me that I had just witnessed an incredible miracle of forgiveness. You see, that young man was the person who had introduced their own son to drugs. Their son was, at that time, still in jail because of the crimes he had committed as a consequence of his drug addiction.

I was both challenged and inspired by this incredible couple. They had found a key to peace. They were free people because they chose to forgive.

How many times?

The Gospel of Matthew records a conversation about forgiveness between Jesus and Peter. Peter asks Jesus a question, and everyone around him is curious to hear the answer:

> Then Peter came to Jesus and asked, 'Lord, how many times shall I forgive my brother or sister who sins against me? Up to seven times?'
>
> Jesus answered, 'I tell you, not seven times, but seventy-seven times' (Matthew 18:21–22).

Peter is asking, 'How many times do I *have* to forgive? The Old Testament Law says seven (which is my obligation).' I'm sure you get where Peter is coming from. Surely there is a limit to how many times I have to forgive some people!

Jesus' message is clear. The number is irrelevant; there is no limit. Don't keep count. Just keep forgiving and make yours a life of forgiveness.

To really drive his point home, Jesus then tells a parable of two servants and a king, recorded in Matthew 18:23–35. What a story!

A king is settling accounts, and discovers a huge debt owed him by a servant. In our terms, it's millions (if not billions) of dollars – an amount that is impossible for the servant to repay. We can only imagine how that debt has accrued. If it wasn't theft, then this fellow is a woeful bookkeeper or terrible investor.

The servant makes an outrageous request of the king: 'Give me time and I will repay you.' However, the king's response is even more outrageous. He shows mercy. He forgives him totally for the debt and sets him free.

You would expect that the servant would leave grateful and be gracious from that day on. But here's what happens. A short time later the servant encounters a co-worker, who we are told owes him a small debt equal to around three months' wages. It's not insignificant, but it is quite possible that his colleague could pay back that amount in instalments. He makes a reasonable request: 'Just give me time to repay.'

The response of the (already) forgiven servant is harsh. He refuses to forgive his colleague and has him thrown in jail until he can repay the debt.

The king hears of this and his response is one of outrage. He has the unforgiving servant bound and thrown into prison.

Here is the net result: the consequence of the unforgiveness of one person means the imprisonment of two. That's exactly what unforgiveness does. It imprisons both the person who is not forgiven and the person who won't forgive.

There's a line in the Lord's Prayer that is similarly challenging: 'And forgive us our debts, as we also have forgiven our debtors' (Matthew 6:12). Some translations use the word 'sin', while others refer to a 'debt'.

The old King James Version uses the word 'trespasses' – or as a little boy prayed, 'trash baskets'. I think it's a good way of looking at it: 'Forgive me for the junk in my life as I forgive the junk that people have dumped on me.'

What a prayer: forgive me, *as* I forgive others. It carries an understanding that you can't live *under* forgiveness without living *out* forgiveness.

On a visit to South Africa some years ago, we visited the historic Robben Island. This was the place where many political prisoners were sent during the horrendous apartheid era in that nation, including Nelson Mandela. After our guide told us that he too had once been a prisoner on the island, a friend of mine asked him, 'Given all you experienced in those years that you were imprisoned here, how can you display such happiness?'

'That's simple,' said our guide. 'When I entered this place, I was an illiterate man, but I learned to read and write, thanks to some of my fellow prisoners'. He then walked across to a cupboard, reached in and grabbed an old, worn Bible. He said, 'We had very little material to read, but we had one of these. Often, our lessons were by candlelight. Once my reading skills improved, I began to read it, and have done so many times since.'

Still holding that old book in his hand, he continued, 'I can summarise this book with one word … and that's the reason I'm a free man today.'

'What's that word?' someone asked.

'Forgiveness,' he replied.

The stories he then told about the encounters that he had with former prison guards, long after he had been released, were gripping. He had forgiven them all and genuinely carried no resentment.

Painful things happen to all of us. People fail, abuse, neglect and betray us – even people who should be the ones to protect us, like our fathers. The big question is: What will we do about it?

People may have caused you to suffer deep wounds, but ultimately there must come a time when the offence does not define you. Don't allow the actions of others, perhaps including your father, to shape the way you see yourself. Say 'No' to allowing other people's actions to define who you are.

Real freedom happens when we step out on the journey of forgiveness. If we don't, unforgiveness imprisons us.

17. Let It Go

Lyn and I once did a cruise along the coast of Alaska. I learned a lot on that trip, especially about icebergs. For example, when we look at an iceberg above water, we're only seeing about 10 per cent of its total volume. The rest is hidden beneath the surface.

Icebergs and people have a lot in common. We seldom know what's happening beneath a person's exterior. We can see things such as their appearance, performance or position, but much of their life, their personality and their character is often hidden from sight.

For some men, what lies underneath includes pain, anger and possibly even the desire for revenge. But as I mentioned in the last chapter, it's important that we don't let the actions of others shape our identity. If we hold on to offence and hurt, it will eventually shape who we are. Ultimately, it will imprison us in a jail of our own making.

The apostle Paul had his fair share of strife, yet he was still able to write the following to his friends in Ephesus: 'Be kind and compassionate to one another, forgiving each other, just as in Christ God forgave you' (Ephesians 4:32).

Signs of unforgiveness

Sometimes it's easy to identify where you are carrying unforgiveness in your life. At other times, it's not so easy to put your finger on the problem. However, there are a number of signs that can help you identify what is going on beneath the surface.

You're on repeat. You just can't stop talking about 'it' or 'them'. The offence and the offender's name are on your lips way too often. Somehow, you seem to include various incidents in conversations, usually without intending to. The reason for that is simple: you are carrying that matter, or disappointment with that person, in your heart. Jesus himself said that 'the mouth speaks what the heart is full of' (Matthew 12:34).

Your 'computer' has a virus. We've all experienced what happens when a virus affects our computer. The computer slows right down and cannot function properly. Unresolved conflict is just like that. It plays on our mind; it bogs us down. The issue is there, under the surface, all the time. Usually, we lose objectivity. Our judgement can become clouded, even biased, particularly where it relates to the one who caused the offence.

Anger. You will probably get mad at God, because you have unrealistic expectations of justice. Actually, you expect him to side with you completely. It seems unfair if the offending party succeeds or is blessed. You will find yourself thinking, 'How can God care for them, after all they did to me?'

Bitterness. Unresolved issues fester under the surface. If the root cause of the pain in your life is not dealt with, the poison can spread and leave you a bitter person. This bitterness will affect everything about you, including your personality and the quality of your relationships. You will never be the person, the husband or the father you could be if you don't let go of disappointments and forgive the things you deem unforgivable.

Spiritual implications

Unresolved issues invite an unwanted enemy into your world. Drawing again from Paul's writings on this subject: "'In your anger do not sin": do not let the sun go down while you are still angry, and do not give the devil a foothold' (Ephesians 4:26–27). Dark forces are capable of infiltrating our lives via the doors of unresolved conflict. Paul is warning us that if we hold on to offence – even overnight, let alone over years – and if we carry unforgiveness, dark forces will start to control more and more of our life.

So the question that we must wrestle with is simply 'How do I forgive so I can move on and live free?' Let's not be glib here. This is a journey. It's where the 'seventy-seven times' factor kicks in (see chapter 16).

But how do I forgive?

I've been in the business of helping people for a long time. Here are some common components of a journey that brings people through to a place of peace, happiness and freedom.

Ask for help

Firstly, you need God's help. He gives grace to those who ask. Grace turns weaknesses into strength. This is important because some of us have been so battered and bruised by hurtful experiences in our past. Knowledge alone is not ability. We can acknowledge our need to forgive, but we may need his strength to activate it. We also need to call on the support of trusted, mature people to walk with us.

Let it go

Give the offence and the offender over to the Lord. Have you ever tried to catch a mad dog with your bare hands? It's really easy to get bitten. If you keep holding on to that thing the wrong way, it will keep biting you. I know that from personal experience. You just have to let some things go. There's no denying how wrong and how hurtful the person was. But you'll never move forward while you hold on to resentment and unforgiveness.

Relinquish your right to get even

This is serious. The desire for vengeance will erode your soul and cause you to become an angry old man. Have you ever said, 'I'll forgive them, but I won't forget what they did'? This may be true, but you can arrive at a place where those memories don't hurt anymore.

There's a difference between a wound and a scar. A wound is something that hasn't healed. There are a lot of men still carrying a father wound. A scar, on the other hand, shows where something painful has happened, but it's finally healed. *Your scars show your victories – and they can actually encourage other men.* If you can get over the pain of your past, it's likely that they can too!

Give it time

Healing is a process. Forgiveness is not a one-off event. Some issues will keep coming up, but you will eventually recover if you commit yourself to keeping your heart in the right place, focusing on the right things in life, and avoiding unhealthy environments.

There used to be pain relief advertisements on television that always ended with great advice: 'If pain persists, see a doctor.' The same might apply to your emotional pain. If so, get professional help from someone like a psychologist or counsellor who can give you support and advice as you walk this path. At the back of this book, there are some resources that can help you get started.

It's also important to understand that forgiveness is not the same as reconciliation. You might forgive the one who caused the offence, but you might not return to same level of relationship. In fact, that might not be possible. Some people shouldn't be afforded the level of trust you showed them before you were hurt by them. Forgiveness *can* happen quickly, but building trust is much slower.

You might be wondering what happens if your father has died. You can still forgive him and be released from your unforgiveness. One option you could consider is to write him a letter. Some men have told me of the benefits of writing letters to their deceased fathers, knowing full well that they can't be received. They report the therapeutic benefits of such an action.

The Japanese art form of *kintsugi* is a wonderful illustration of what God can do for a broken life. The artist does not throw away broken pottery, choosing instead to use it to create something magnificent. There is respect for the history of the original object. The imperfections are embraced rather than causing the object to be discarded. Through the skill of the artisan, the broken pieces are meticulously reassembled. The strength of the object no longer comes from its own substance: the renewed vessel has its broken pieces joined together with gold. Once completed, the object is of far greater worth than it was originally.

We've all got a few scars. Obviously, each scar has a story of pain we've experienced. There's another way of looking at the scars of our lives, though. Following God's healing, we are renewed vessels, put back together again with seams of gold that now exist where there was once brokenness. Every gram of the gold represents another act of God's divine love that has been applied to our life.

Reposition yourself

Have you ever noticed that the windscreen in a car is much larger than the rear-view mirror? It's a metaphor. We're meant to spend a lot more time looking forward than back.

I made that discovery at my first-ever school athletics carnival. I represented my small country school in the Year 1 sprint race. I got a great start. In fact, halfway down the track I was way out in front … until I had the dumbest idea: 'I should look around to see where everyone else is.' Well, that didn't go well! More than half the field passed me over the next few metres. It wasn't my finest sporting moment.

I learned a lesson that day: if you want to win at anything in life, you have to live with a forward focus. The apostle Paul had a great philosophy: 'forgetting what is behind … I press on …' (Philippians 3:13–14). Pressing on demands looking forward.

Stuff happens. We wish it didn't. It's wrong and can be very painful. You can't change your past, but you can change your future – through decisions you make today. There is no more important decision than to forgive.

Was there ever anything more brutal than what Jesus Christ endured on a cruel Roman cross, and in the hours leading up to his crucifixion? The betrayal, the beatings, the humiliation, the agony of it all is impossible to comprehend. But to our amazement, with his last few breaths, he still cried, 'Father, forgive them, for they do not know what they are doing' (Luke 23:34).

Take a moment to reflect on that …

Jesus could have called on heaven's armies. That's vengeance. It would have been justified. But he chose forgiveness instead. Today, we live in the benefit of that choice.

PART 5

A Better Man

Introduction

'I thought you were Ironman. I can't believe this is you.'

These were the words of a junior staff member who watched me sob uncontrollably in the office. I couldn't believe it was me either. I'd spent my entire adult life thinking that this type of crisis never happened to people like me. But it does ... and it did.

Perhaps I should've seen it coming, but I was blindsided. That moment when I cracked was the culmination of a series of events and circumstances over a prolonged period of time. For once in my life, I felt like I was completely out of control. I was physically exhausted yet unable to sleep. I was overwhelmed with an intense sense of helplessness. An avalanche of emotions poured out. And I finally admitted that I was soul-weary.

Fortunately, we caught things long before they got to a point of no return. That is only thanks to God's grace and an amazing wife and family, plus the support of some great mates and mentors.

This whole experience, however, started me on a journey of discovery to learn more about myself and what I need to keep going. I found a fresh resolve to never lose sight of the important things in life, like the joy and peace that comes from having margins. I'm also more motivated than ever to teach a new generation of leaders important principles to avoid similar pitfalls.

It's good to find moments to re-evaluate our lifestyle, our relationships, and our inner world, and then have the courage to make the necessary adjustments that will lead us to be healthier in every way. I'm sure you join me in saying:

- I want to be a loving husband.
- I want to be a great dad.
- I want to be a generous friend.
- I want to make a difference in my world.
- I want to be *a better man.*

18. The Comeback

Aussies love a good comeback – especially in sport. Take Kieren Perkins, for example, in the 1996 Olympics. He won the gold medal in the 1500 metre freestyle swimming event from lane eight, the lane of the slowest qualifier. I still remember where I was as I listened to that race, and how impressed I was with his superhuman effort. It was a comeback for the ages.

It's time to turn the focus to men who feel like they are the ones who've failed – men who need to make a 'comeback'. For all of us, regardless of our past or present reality, it's time to make the choice to become a better man.

There's one common thing every human being shares: we've all made mistakes. We've all failed. I often tell people that if they feel that they are perfect, we would appreciate them flying around the room while we give them a little clap!

So it's good to know that comebacks are what the kingdom of God is all about. There's a classic story in Scripture that illustrates this point well in John chapter 21 – you may want to read it for yourself (see vv. 3–17). It's the story of Jesus reinstating Peter.

The narrative is primarily between Jesus and Peter, but there are six other men there. It's always good to ask yourself, when reading the Bible: 'Where am I in this picture?'

It's set on the shores of the Sea of Galilee. I have stood there myself a number of times and tried to imagine some of these Bible stories unfolding right there. On this occasion, Peter is in a personal crisis of faith. You may remember that he was the guy who had denied knowing Jesus (not just once, but three times!). You could say he was a repeat offender.

He decides to go fishing. It is an unsuccessful venture until Jesus enters the scene, encouraging Peter and his friends to try a different approach. This results in them catching 153 large fish. By the time they reach the shore, Jesus has already cooked breakfast. Like so many occasions in Jesus' ministry, he gives them life-changing truths not from a platform, but over a meal.

Then a conversation begins between Peter and the Messiah. Ultimately, healing flows into the life of a man who has felt like such a failure.

I'd like to draw your attention to three statements recorded in the story.

'I'm going out to fish'

Peter feels like a failure. He's failed God. He's denied Jesus and he feels like a coward. It's fair to assume that he is disgusted with himself. So he decides to go back to what he once was.

The worst time to make major decisions is when you're tired, broke or sick, or when you feel like you have failed in some significant area. Conclusions reached in these times are usually based on our preservation (at best), rather than our destiny. Without exception, those decisions will cause us to retreat, never advance.

Peter feels so low. We can get so discouraged and dark emotionally that we influence others negatively, and negativity is more infectious than the flu! When Peter says, 'I'm going out to fish,' the others say, 'We'll go with you.' At times like this, everything seems futile. What do they catch? Like us on a lot of our fishing trips – nothing!

On return from a trip to Papua New Guinea with symptoms similar to malaria, I was placed in hospital as soon as I arrived home. A fever raged. My energy stocks were almost non-existent and I was frustrated.

Lyn came to visit me the day after I was hospitalised. Her first question was simply, 'What have you been doing?'

'Thinking,' I muttered in reply.

'About what?' she further enquired.

'What I do after I quit this lifestyle – travelling and preaching.'

I expected bucketloads of compassion to be poured over my weary soul. But no, that didn't happen. She simply stood up, smiled, and turned to leave the ward. Before she left, she gave me something else to process. 'You have a fever. You are delirious. I will come back when you're thinking straight.'

I'm so grateful for a wife who did not join my pity party that day. Needless to say, I did not quit, and I'm still happily doing what I feel called to do, decades later.

Peter and I have a lot in common.

'Come and have breakfast'

Into the scene comes Jesus Christ, walking into a life damaged by Peter's own mistakes. He knows Peter isn't a bad man, just somebody who has done a bad thing.

How does he restore him? Not with a sermon, delving into deep spiritual truths. (Exploring the significance of the curtains and colours in the tabernacle isn't relevant here.) Jesus is practical. He serves Peter. He seems to know that the way to this fisherman's heart is through his belly.

Actions pierce hard hearts. Sometimes words just bounce off people's ears when a simple act of compassion can send a powerful message. Imagine the Son of God cooking breakfast for people who have let him down so badly … and then inviting them to dine. That sounds a lot like the communion table to me!

'Do you love me?'

After breakfast, Jesus asks Peter a question. Many hearing this story for the first time would expect a tirade of rebuke from Jesus, like 'You let me down', 'I'm disappointed in you', or 'Do you know how that made me feel?'

But that's not what Jesus does. He doesn't even mention Peter's denials. Instead he asks, 'Simon son of John, do you love me?' He asks this question three times – the same number of times Peter denied knowing Jesus.

All three times, Peter replies that he loves him, and Jesus' response is to give him a new job – to invite Peter to look to the future, not the past – pointing out what he can be, rather than what he has done.

Jesus leads Peter to restoration: first back into relationship with him, and then back into service of his God. Peter's focus shifts from his mistakes to his Master, who has spoken words of confidence like these into Peter's life: 'I trust you, Peter. You're not a failure. You have a future in which you will help people and bring glory to my name.'

A few chapters later, in the book of Acts, we find Peter preaching the first sermon of the early church on the day of Pentecost. What a comeback!

Can you imagine being one of Peter's six friends on the shore of the Sea of Galilee that day, watching on? Right in front of them, they see the risen Saviour at work, pouring out his love, grace and kindness on a fallen human being.

The challenge is for us to see every human being the way Jesus does – an image bearer of the Creator of the universe. That should cause us to see people differently … not as problems, failures, damaged or dirty, but as potential recipients of God's redemptive grace.

Jesus didn't rub Peter's nose in the consequences of his sins and failures. In fact, he didn't mention them. We recite our past, but Jesus redeems it. And like the apostle Paul, we can joyfully announce with confidence, 'Therefore, there is now no condemnation for those who are in Christ Jesus' (Romans 8:1).

Are you ready to make a comeback? Are you ready to be a better man?

19. A Better Husband

One of the great voices to men in the twentieth century was Edwin Louis Cole. He is famously quoted as saying: 'Being a male is a matter of birth. Being a man is a matter of choice.'

There is a real identity crisis in today's society regarding what it means to be a man. We need to embrace the challenge of redefining it in a proper, wholesome and biblical way.

Being a better man starts by understanding what it means to be a real man. Unlike some of the images that are portrayed in the movies or on social media platforms, our manhood has nothing to do with what's on the outside. We've all met some males with big muscles who turn out to be really weak men.

A real man knows how to be courageous. He does what's right, rather than just what's popular.

A real man takes responsibility for the spiritual and emotional climate in his home. He's given up playing the blame game. He takes ownership of his attitudes and actions.

A real man knows how to give honour where honour is due, especially to that uniquely gifted individual who is his wife.

And *a real man is an adult.* He is mature. He's grown beyond the immaturity that expresses itself through selfishness, and he has learned to put others first.

Every home needs a roof to provide a covering to protect it from the elements. Parents also provide a covering. When the relationship between mum and dad is strong, children living under that influence benefit greatly. Not only is a wonderful example being set for them, but it also creates a sense of safety and security in their growing years.

I've conducted many weddings over the years. It's always a day of celebration where two individuals, full of hopes and dreams, make solemn vows to commit to each other, and have the potential to build something great. This book isn't about marriage. There is plenty of great material available to anyone who wants to invest in this special and sacred relationship. However, we can't address the issue of healing generations without discussing marriage.

Husbands, one of the greatest things you can do for your children is to love your wife unreservedly. Studies have shown that children feel safe in families where the mum and dad love each other.

We were never created to do life alone. I want to invite you to explore a striking parallel that the Bible gives between Christ's love for the church and the love that is expected of a husband towards his wife: 'Husbands, love your wives, just as Christ loved the church and gave himself up for her' (Ephesians 5:25).

Question: How did Jesus love the church?

Answer: He was selfless, sincere and sacrificial.

There are far too many women who have had the joy of life crushed out of them because they were told by their husband (who has taken Scripture out of context) to submit to his leadership in the home.

A friend of mine, whose ministry is specifically with men in domestic family violence situations, has helped me understand the reasons for this kind of behaviour. His insights may help you or somebody you know.

He told me this:

A lot of men want respect, but they don't understand that they have to earn it. They think it is one of their rights, assuming a wedding ring gives them the right to demand respect. Some men have a flawed, if not toxic, view of being 'the head of the house'. They expect respect automatically. Because they don't have any idea how to earn it, the closest counterfeit to respect is fear. You see, if I don't know how to make you respect me, I will attempt to make you fear me and that feels close enough.

He continued:

Thankfully, there is hope for these relationships as long as there is substance to that hope. It's not just fingers crossed, expecting things will be better. Hope based on substance looks like knowing why change is going to happen (a decision), and what you've changed (behavioural patterns).

There are some excellent tools to help men change their responses, especially in the area of anger management. One of the wisest choices you'll ever make is to seek help, and learn the skills necessary to bring healing to your marriage. Finally, you've got to have accountability around those choices if you are to change and show the genuine fruit of change.

The Bible calls Jesus the King of kings, and yet he clearly demonstrated that he did not come to be served, but rather to serve. If we are going to take this journey as followers of Christ, then we need to make him our benchmark and serve those we love.

The challenge for each of us is to be a man whose wife respects him. Respect is what others give you because you give them an example. It cannot be demanded; and, like a bank account, it is built up over a long time via small deposits.

I want to be respected, especially by my wife. It actually matters more to me than being successful. I've noticed that success for some men comes at a price that I'm just not prepared to pay.

There comes a time in the life of reasonably minded men when they realise that it's way more important to be respected by their families than to be admired by others for their perceived success.

The Bible asks a very important question: 'What good is it for someone to gain the whole world, yet forfeit their soul?' (Mark 8:36). We all know men who have all the trinkets of success, and yet in the pursuit of that success they have forfeited their soul – the man on the inside. It's just not worth it!

You can earn greater respect from your wife than you enjoy right now. But some things will need to change. Here's how it starts. Look at the man in the mirror and tell him, 'A better us starts with a better me.' Then take the following steps.

Be a better communicator

There's a simple pattern in communication. Someone speaks while someone else listens, the latter getting an opportunity eventually to respond.

I'm not sure who does the counting in those academic studies, but we are told that women use around 31,000 words a day. Some suggest that men use 4,000 fewer than that per day. But that's not the point.

You do the maths. Your wife will use one million words every month. And here's the good news … she's saving some of them just for you! You need to hear her views before making major decisions. The times I have frustrated Lyn the most have been times when she has thought I wasn't listening. Guys, we have to admit that most of us are not great listeners, but if we learn to respect our wife's perspective, we will reap the rewards.

A lot of marriages would improve markedly if husbands learned one important skill – listening with their eyes. Focus. Resist the urge to respond quickly – to solve your wife's problems, or point out where she is wrong. Just sit and listen.

A second important skill is learning to speak from our heart. Most of us aren't terribly eloquent, but that's okay. Your wife isn't looking for an orator; she wants a soulmate. It's a huge step for some men to begin to share their feelings, but it is a step worth taking. With every new level of vulnerability, you will discover a new level of intimacy in your marriage.

We also need to understand the power that's in the words we use. The Bible has much to say about the power of our words.

In Proverbs, we read 'The tongue has the power of life and death …' (Proverbs 18:21). Our speech can be creative or destructive: it can build up or pull down.

Jesus said that 'the mouth speaks what the heart is full of' (Luke 6:45). So it's not really a speech problem that we have, but a heart problem. Our daily prayer should be, 'God, renew my heart, so that no matter what pressure I'm under, only life-giving words flow out of me.'

No wonder James wrote to the early church believers, 'My dear brothers and sisters, take note of this: everyone should be quick to listen, slow to speak and slow to become angry' (James 1:19).

Such wisdom. Be quick to listen and slow to speak … because the wrong words are like fuel on simmering coals, causing explosions that create uncontrollable, destructive fires.

If you can grow in those two areas – listening with your eyes and speaking from your heart – you'll discover some amazing things. Conflicts can be resolved. Dreams can be awakened. Opportunities can be discovered. And most importantly of all, your marriage will be enriched.

Be a better romantic

For some men, the most romantic line they'll ever use is 'Are you awake?' It's not really smooth, is it?

One of the most endearing sights to see is an old couple walking together holding hands. They have obviously kept the spark of love alive many years after their honeymoon. And you can too.

A healthy love life does not start behind the bedroom door. It starts by showing warmth, kindness and affection every day. Little things matter. They include remembering special dates like birthdays and anniversaries; attending to practical matters around the home; keeping your promises; and being thoughtful. It sounds a lot like loving your wife in a sacrificial, selfless (Jesus) kind of way.

Some of the best advice I was ever given was to find out my wife's love language – to know the ways she receives my heartfelt love for her. Because if she doesn't understand, my message may be missed. Let me illustrate this.

I attended a service for Chinese believers some years back. Almost the entire service was in Mandarin. The only word I understood was 'Hallelujah'. Like that famous skit with Mr Bean, I energetically joined them in song with that one word, because I simply did not understand anything else that was being said or sung. I just didn't understand their language.

But you will do yourself a huge favour by discovering your wife's love language – the ways in which your wife feels most affirmed in her relationship with you. If she is the practical type, don't bother getting fresh if you failed to help with the washing up or bathing the children. Trust me: it's important ... I may have learned that the hard way!

A word of caution ...

We have acknowledged throughout this book that a significant percentage of marriages fail. If you are currently separated or divorced, be wise in the way you speak to your children about their mother.

The Bible commands us to honour our mother and father – and promises God's blessing to those who do. Remember that as the father of impressionable young people, you have no right to undermine their love and respect for their mum. And you definitely have no right to create a wedge in those important relationships. Despite your current pain, ask God to help you maintain a gracious demeanour towards the mother of your children.

May God give you great wisdom in this area. And may you know healing and restoration at whatever level is possible in your relationship with your former or estranged partner.

20. A Better Dad

The story is told of a man who, many years ago, travelled far and wide to present his well-packaged talk titled 'Ten Commandments for Parents'. Crowds would gather to hear this orator eloquently expound the skills necessary to successfully raise well-balanced children. As things turned out, this man fell in love and married. Then his first child came along. The title was eventually changed to 'A Few Suggestions for Parents'. Rumour has it that after welcoming their third child into the family, he was never heard of again.

Parenting, though not easy, is undeniably rewarding. It requires wisdom, grace, patience, strength and energy – all in liberal doses. Being a father brings incredible joy. But it also carries great responsibilities, one of which is to find ways to regularly express to our children the three big messages that are the heartbeat of this book: 'You are my child. I love you. I'm proud of you.'

We saw earlier how God the Father demonstrated his love to his Son in that way. Now, through the Son, he shows it to us. Having freely received his love, we are able to freely give this great gift to the generation following us.

In a church service on Father's Day in 2002, I took the opportunity to honour my father. I led him to the front and seated him on a lounge chair on the stage, while I preached a message about him … and to him. It was titled 'Ten Things You Have Taught Me'.

Here is a summary of those 10 life lessons:

1. People do look at the outside, even if God looks at the heart. Some people say don't judge a book by its cover, but people do. So clean your shoes and iron your shirt!

2. A person's character is more important than the titles they gain or the bank balance they accrue. A good name is better than riches.

3. Tortoises can win races. They can even beat flashy hares. So just keep doing the right things and who knows …

4. A bad start in life doesn't have to mean a bad finish. Plan to keep growing.

5. Never neglect the little guy. Be committed to giving everyone a fair go.

6. The best things in life really are free. Sunrises. Walks on the beach. A few kind words.

7. You don't have to see everything. Practise 'selective blindness' with your children, and don't react to every little misdemeanour.

8. Love with an open hand. Surrender the desire to be a control freak.

9. Be tenacious in prayer. Stay in partnership with the God who cares for your kids more than you do. Commit them to him daily.

10. Serve God with all your heart. It's the only way to live.

Later, my mother told me that on the way home from that church service, my father went rather quiet in the car. When she asked if there was a problem, he burst out with, 'That's the nicest thing that blooming idiot ever did for me.'

After that Father's Day, the years rolled on. In 2015, my mother's health deteriorated rapidly after a series of strokes. My parents moved into an aged-care facility. There, I watched this dear old man read the Bible, pray and even sing praise songs to his wife of over sixty years. He showed me what it was to honour your marriage vows – for better for worse … in sickness and in health … till death us do part.

My father wasn't a millionaire, but I'm a wealthy man because of his legacy. And I, in turn, make sure that my children know the very same thing.

The Bible says, 'A good man leaves an inheritance to his children's children' (Proverbs 13:22 NKJV). What legacy do you want to leave? Start today by taking intentional steps to be a better dad.

There are certain things that we can do to practically demonstrate our love to our children. Here are some of the important ones.

Listen to them

The psalms of King David give us wonderful reflections. He wrote:

> I am passionately in love with God because he listens to me. He hears my prayers and answers them. As long as I live I'll keep praying to him, for he stoops down to listen to my heart's cry (Psalm 116:1–2).[1]

David portrays God as one who shows his love for, and genuine interest in, him by stooping down to hear him. It's a magnificent picture that he paints of a father inclining his ear to his son.

I spent a lot of my younger years subjecting my ears to loud rock music. I loved it, but it may have slightly impaired my hearing. These days, when little children like my grandkids want to tell me something important I find it necessary to get down to their level so that I don't miss the important things they want to say to me. You can tell that it matters to them.

When was the last time that you got down to the level of your children and genuinely listened to them? Let me suggest that there are a few things they may want to say to you, like:

- 'Please respect my individuality.'
- 'I'm anxious.'
- 'Lighten up.'
- 'Can we just hang out together?'

You will miss those important messages if you don't intentionally stop, stoop and listen with your undivided attention.

Teach them

The Bible encourages us to 'Dedicate your children to God and point them in the way that they should go, and the values they've learned from you will be with them for life' (Proverbs 22:6).[2]

That kind of instruction demands a question: What are we teaching our kids?

There is a strong possibility that they won't thank you for all of your instruction when they are going through their teenage years, but when they reflect back as adults, they will be grateful for the principles you taught them.

My good friend Joel Chelliah produced a book for fathers, to help them with conversations with their sons about sexuality.

It's called *The Chat.*[3] When it was first published, I asked him why he wrote it. I was inspired by his reply:

> I'm a father of three boys. When it came to the time when we needed to have 'the chat' and discuss issues about sex and sexuality, I realised there was a gap in resources that I felt were suitable for this purpose. I really wanted to be the first voice in this conversation about the subject – not the second voice, having to correct what I considered error.

> So I wrote something specifically for boys only – innocent, yet clear enough to have a conversation at seven to eight years of age. It provides a platform for questions that young boys want to ask, and then be answered without shame. The Chat is not a textbook. It's an opportunity for fathers to start a conversation.

Set them boundaries

Many years ago, we were part of a team that established a home for young women who were, for various reasons, in need of support. It's been very successful and continues to help many people decades after opening its doors.

We had a situation in the early days when we were called to the house due to a commotion that was happening onsite. I discovered that one of our residents had stolen some property. The owner had come to the facility, demanding it back. Things had deteriorated quickly after that.

Having regained some semblance of order, I took the young woman aside and let her know how she had failed, and how she had put every resident in that facility at risk due to her actions. Once we had finished our meeting, I noticed that she had become emotional. When I asked why she was upset, she looked at me with a heightened sense of gratitude and said, 'Nobody ever loved me enough to speak to me like that. I now know you genuinely care for me.'

Young people need to know boundaries. Some behaviour is unacceptable. Some activities are unsafe. Some attitudes are detrimental to their wellbeing and the environment of the family home. It's your job to determine where the lines that should not be crossed are. Set boundaries and identify consequences for ignoring them. Wise parents do this when things are calm, long before things get out of control.

Be there

A wise old man once gave me some excellent advice: 'Waste time with the people you love.' Possibly the most common regret of most fathers, myself included, is that they have allowed the demands of life to rob them of quality time with their children.

We are all capable of fixing that situation. It's really not complicated. Everyone gets the same amount of time available to them every day – 1,440 minutes. Our priorities will determine how we use them.

My dad was a bi-vocational pastor. He was busy when I was growing up, working Monday to Friday in a secular job and then pastoring a small local church in the evenings and on weekends. Despite all that, I never felt that I lacked access to him, because he would go out of his way to make sure I knew that he was there for me. He was particularly good at showing that in the little things.

During the school holidays, he would swing by the house while he was driving a truck to see if I wanted to join him. I spent a lot of time sitting in the front seat of that plumbing supplies delivery truck, feeling like the king of the world. We didn't always talk a lot. Just being there was enough.

I remember one occasion when he skipped church on a Sunday to come and watch me play in a tennis competition. I didn't know he was coming until I walked onto the court and saw him there. It was quite a shock, because in those days, he was not a fan of Christians playing sport on Sunday. Sadly, we lost the final in a close game; but that doesn't really matter, because etched in my memory is an image of my father in the crowd. It was a sacrifice for him. I understood that. Even in my turbulent teen years, I knew he was showing me unconditional love.

Here's something I tell young dads in particular: if you want to spend time with your sons, get a focal point for your good intentions. Get something that will remind you to do activities with them. It could be a cheap tent, a surfboard, a gym membership or a boat. Whatever it is, make sure it is something that you can do together. One father told me, 'I took your advice, and I feel like I've got my son back.'

Be consistent

It was my incredible honour to conduct the funeral of my friend, mentor and former leader a few years ago. He was a man of significant profile in our nation, having filled a number of important leadership roles. Tributes flowed for the great man. But the greatest compliment of all came from his oldest son, who unashamedly declared, 'My father was the most consistent man I know. He was the same in our backyard at home as he was standing on stage, speaking to thousands.'

When it comes to parenting, consistency is a superpower. In the words of a popular quote, 'Your actions speak so loudly, I cannot hear what you are saying.'[4]

The apostle Paul put it this way in 2 Corinthians 3:2: 'You yourselves are our letter, written on our hearts, known and read by everyone.' In simple terms, your life is an open book. Your son will do what his dad *does* way more than what his dad *says*. So be consistent.

I don't recall ever meeting anyone who has made the decision to regress in life. At the core of our being there's a strong desire to do better – to be better. Rarely does this happen in isolation. We have to access places and spaces where progress, growth and healing can occur.

21. Mentors and Mates

Mentors

His name was Bob. He wasn't cool. He wasn't fashionable. He was, in every way, a very ordinary person, imperfect in lots of ways like the rest of us. But there are few people who significantly influenced my life in my early teenage years compared to him.

Looking back, I have realised that Bob played an important part in building foundations that would ultimately help me make quality decisions in my adulthood. We never gave him a title back then, but we have terminology now for what people like Bob do to help boys become men, and men become better men. He was a mentor.

There was a small group of about six lads who would regularly go to Bob's house on a Saturday afternoon. He taught us basic mechanics. One time, he let us pull his functioning lawnmower apart and then showed us how to put it back together. I have a funny feeling that he made many adjustments to that motor after we went home, because there were several parts left over when we finished. We raced a go-kart on the allotment at the back of his family home, and built a five-metre-long Canadian canoe which turned out brilliantly.

Bob would pray for us. He encouraged us. At exam time, we would get a short phone call to tell us that he knew that we would do well. He even listened to 14-year-olds tell their stories of failed love. People say it's only puppy love. It is, but it's real to the puppies. He just seemed to know that.

I moved on to another season of life, eventually relocating to another city. Roll the clock forward 20 years, and Lyn and I were attending the opening of a new church facility in our city. At one point, I went for a walk and saw a man serving refreshments to the guests. To my surprise, that man was Bob.

As we caught up, he told me that he'd been following my progress and was very proud of me. At that moment it suddenly dawned on me: I was the man that I was because of God's goodness, praying parents, a few very tolerant people … and this man, Bob.

Sadly, the years hadn't been kind to Bob and he suffered from all kinds of health problems. But he was still the Bob I remembered. Right there and then, I apologised for not thanking him earlier for the incredible input he'd given me years earlier. I got quite emotional. It was a special moment for both of us.

Several years later, I had the honour of conducting my mentor's funeral. Someone commented that it doesn't take long for people like Bob to be forgotten. My response was that while I'm alive, his memory will live on, and his legacy, through me, will be lived out.

The apostle Paul writes that even if one has 10,000 teachers or guardians in Christ, one does not have many fathers (1 Corinthians 4:15). Paul wasn't speaking about a connection that was biological; rather, he was talking about something on a very different level. He knew that:

- Teachers give their lessons – but fathers give their lives.
- Teachers have information – but fathers have influence.

The need for mentors

Jason has done very well in business over the years. Listen to him talk, and you'll realise he's generating income so he can do what he's passionate about – helping men, especially those who are struggling in life.

Starting as a youth leader, Jason realised that young men needed someone to bounce ideas off. Some of the young men he talks to have great fathers. They are off to a flying start in life. There's just added strength and support having someone else in their corner. Good dads know that it's a wonderful addition to their parenting responsibilities to have a trusted 'other voice' to help guide their sons in the formation of their personhood. This could be a youth leader, an uncle, or a man of proven character in their wider sphere.

And for those whose fathers have been absent or abusive, this is imperative. Jason discovered this through his years of working in youth correctional centres and then in drug rehabilitation facilities. He realised what seems normal to people who had a healthy childhood and were doing well in life was not normal for so many others. So he became a mentor, almost by accident, and has been doing it for over 30 years.

The reason he started his mentoring journey was simple: 'There was a need.' Now, mentoring is one of the things that gives Jason's life purpose and meaning: watching incremental changes happen as men take small steps towards a better life by letting go of things such as anger and destructive behaviours.

Jason took delight in showing me some text messages from people who currently benefit from his support. There were common themes. He listened. He cared. He was trustworthy.

In a world where an increasing number of us are self-obsessed, these are rare but necessary commodities.

The phone rang during our conversation. It was Jimmy. I encouraged Jason to answer. At the completion of the call, his eyes lit up as he told me how much progress Jimmy, now 25 years of age, had made in the decade during which he'd been helping him. 'It's the little wins that are so special,' said Jason of this young man who had come from a broken home. This life-giving arrangement had helped Jimmy to develop skills ranging from changing spark plugs in his car to maintaining a healthy relationship with his wife.

I'm convinced that a lot more mature-aged men could make a positive contribution to the lives of the next generation if we made ourselves available. We just need to realise that we've got a lot to offer.

When your mentor becomes your dad

Oliver is a miracle. By the time he was 15, his life had completely hit rock bottom. Life at home was rough. Mum had disabilities, and his siblings were in trouble with the law. They had joined the drug culture, with all that it entailed. There was no man in the family, and he had no-one he could call 'Dad'.

With no hope for the future, Oliver attempted suicide. This young man was 190 cm tall and weighed only 50 kilograms. It was decided to hospitalise him, and it was around that time that things began to turn around.

A young Christian girl encouraged Oliver to do something radical: 'Get on a train and go to Windsor station. There will be a man waiting there who you've never met before. He will help you.' That man was an active member of our church. His name is Allan.

This mature man, with a family of his own, showed Oliver unconditional love – something he'd never experienced before. 'He showed me a completely different way to live,' says Oliver. 'I discovered a true father's heart, that constantly demonstrates that it doesn't matter what a son does, because the father's love does not change.'

There was no official agreement between them, just an open door and a lot of kindness shown to this hurting teenager. Now an adult and married with children of his own, Oliver has made some important observations. 'Growing up, you need good reference points to show you what you can become as a man. Without them, everything is skewed,' he told me.

There's a magnificent twist to this story. Oliver realised a number of years ago how important a name is. When he decided to marry the special lady in his life, he wanted to go into that new era carrying a name that meant something to him. He wanted the children who would be raised in his family to carry a name that they would be proud of. For several years, he had called Allan 'Dad'. To honour him, and to redefine a new family culture, on his wedding day Oliver chose to change his surname officially, adopting the name of the man he'll always call 'Dad'.

I shared my thoughts about this with a respected leader of a national men's program over breakfast in an inner-city café. We discussed the need for men to have someone in their life who will support and encourage them, and hold them accountable. 'Men need mentors and mates,' I suggested. This wise and seasoned sage agreed, but added one other important ingredient to the mix: 'And a band of brothers.'

Mates

If you are not from Australia, you may not be familiar with the concept of 'mates'. Let me explain. They are special people who you trust. They are reliable. And they've got your back.

Our nation rightly stops every year on 25 April to remember with gratitude the feats and sacrifices of a group of people known as the Anzacs (Australian and New Zealand Army Corps). Brave men and women like these Anzac soldiers have, through our short history, punched above their weight in theatres of war.

In doing so, they have not only protected our nation, but have liberated others, despite often being outnumbered and under-resourced. When you examine the Anzac culture, you come to realise what motivates and strengthens our servicemen and women. The stated Anzac values are endurance, courage, ingenuity, good humour and mateship. To face the battles of life with a trusted mate at your side is a gamechanger compared with facing tough times alone.

We've all got battles. We've all got an enemy of some sort that we need to beat. Don't fight alone. Get a friend who will stand with you and join you in the fight … similar to Jonathan's armour-bearer in the Bible, who told his friend Jonathan, 'I am with you heart and soul' (1 Samuel 14:7). This is a classic Old Testament battlefield story, of a prince named Jonathan and his nameless armour-bearer. (If you are a golfer, he's like a caddy.) It's worth a read in 1 Samuel 14, but let me give you a short summary.

While the king and 600 trained men were pontificating under a tree, these two young guys thought they would pick a fight. It's obvious from the text that they weren't certain of victory. They just decided that they didn't want to die wondering.

You knew it would be a lot of fun when Jonathon decided on his course of action … but Scripture tells us that he did not tell his father. (How many of us have got some great stories that we told Dad well *after* the adventure?) They had a battle plan that you won't find in material on successful military strategy. It was simple. Let the enemy see them, and then see what happened next. Amazingly, however, from the outset they started to defeat the enemy.

As a result, the army was mobilised; cowards who had given up found strength to fight again; and ultimately the battle was won. This was all because two mates had a go.

King Solomon wrote the book of Ecclesiastes. He makes an insightful statement in verse 9 of chapter 4: 'Two are better than one.'

Here are some things that a good mate can give you.

Perspective. If you've ever looked out the window of a plane, you'll notice that everything below looks smaller when you're up in the sky. That's the same with relationships. When someone is not directly involved, not up close or consumed with issues, they have different points of reference. Not everything seems so big to them.

Support. When God created the world, he repeatedly said that the things he made were 'good' (Genesis 1–2). The first thing that

God said was '*not* good' was a man on his own (Genesis 2:18). We are so much more effective when someone's at our side than we are alone.

I love the thought that most miracles start with a simple question: 'How can I help you?' The problem for most men is we're just not good at asking for help … or even admitting that we need it.

Accountability. A man called John has some great advice: 'But if we walk in the light, as he is in the light, we have fellowship with one another, and the blood of Jesus, his Son, purifies us from all sin' (1 John 1:7).

As part of my tertiary studies many years ago, I learned how a lot of disease-causing germs are destroyed – by bringing them into the light. Many things that are damaging in our lives can be dealt a deathblow if we will only tell a mature, trusted friend. We never get better when we hide our problems.

Improvement. There's a very simple principle that I've seen demonstrated over and over: you become like the company you keep. So hang around people who you want to be like. Here's a thought from King Solomon on the rewards of your companions: 'Walk with the wise and become wise, for a companion of fools suffers harm' (Proverbs 13:20).

A special mate

He never carried many titles during his life, nor did he ever claim the spotlight. Yet his funeral was huge, by any measure. 'Youngie', as he was affectionately known, was one of those larger-than-life characters – inappropriate at times (there were many times I had to tell this big guy not to wear his lycra bike shorts into my office!), but always without guile.

Performing that funeral was one of the most difficult tasks I've ever had to undertake. I had known Youngie for 40 years, and he was one of the people most instrumental in my coming to faith in Christ. It was a little hard to believe that he was gone at just 60 years of age.

I've led many funeral services throughout my life but there was something very special about this one. It wasn't just the number of people who gathered to honour this special man. There was a tone of gratitude that filled the atmosphere.

At the end of the service, people gathered to support the family and share their special memories of Youngie. I moved among the crowd, and in the process, did a little investigation. Then it dawned on me. I discovered why so many people had gathered to celebrate this seemingly ordinary Aussie guy. When people were asked why they chose to be at that service, overwhelmingly the most common response was 'Every time I met him, he encouraged me.'

We all need someone who has our back and encourages us. Who are you encouraging at the moment? Who is encouraging you? Who is holding you accountable to those life defining decisions you made?

Mates really do make a difference!

22. Community

Mother Teresa described loneliness as 'the most terrible poverty.'[5] Social media has not provided a cure for loneliness. In fact, it has hidden the profound issue that we have in society today: people are more alone than ever. But we were built for community.

I think it's time we had a fresh look at the church of Jesus Christ. It's had a lot of bad publicity in recent times. I admit that it's not perfect. Granted, there have been failures and shortcomings. None of them can be justified. But the vast majority of churches are wonderful communities filled with people who are seeking to know God and serve others. Furthermore, the church is still God's plan for showing his love to a lost and hurting world.

The church is the best place to be when you're having your worst day

There have been a number of occasions when I have looked out across a congregation and seen people worshipping only days after someone special in their life has passed away. The presence of the Father is often more real to us in those moments:

- When we feel the shock waves of a medical diagnosis
- When we feel like we're drowning in trouble in a business
- When strife seems to dominate our lives.

These are the times we need to run *to* God's house, the church, not *away* from it.

Having just celebrated the beauty of the Old Testament temple, David writes something that illustrates this subject: 'For in the day of trouble he will keep me safe in his dwelling …' (Psalm 27:5).

The church is designed to be a hospital

God designed the church to be a community of grace where his Spirit is radically at work. It's a place where healing happens.

If you arrive at a hospital, the medical staff aren't shocked by the pain or the symptoms of your condition. Broken humanity is what they are there for. The Lord alone is our healer, but he has some wonderful support crew: pastors, priests, leaders, and mature people who will stand with you, believing always, for better days ahead.

Struggles. Addictions. Failures. Heartache. He can heal them all. God's healing centre is the church – the place to find both the power of God to change you and the people of God to support you.

The church is meant to be family

It's in that place that you can find the mums and dads, the brothers and sisters, the uncles and aunts whom you long for.

God's heart has always been for lonely people: the displaced and the abandoned, the widow and the orphan. Psalm 68:5 presents that clearly: 'A father to the fatherless, a defender of widows, is God in his holy dwelling.' And knowing that we need to experience love in human form, God's response to the lonely is found in the next verse: 'God sets the lonely in families' (Psalm 68:6).

If you have had a negative experience in a particular church in your past, let me encourage you to pray and ask God to guide you to a safe place where you will find acceptance, kindness and support.

Terry told his story in graphic detail in chapter 2. Who he is today is the result of God's grace, a loving wife, and a life-giving church family.

Terry's story (continued)
'It was the first time I'd told anyone about my past.'

I was in my mid-twenties when my wife forced me to tell the truth. She was getting over my three-day 'benders', so she gave me an ultimatum. It was the first time in my life I'd told anyone about my past. I gave her the warts and all version of me. My wife was pretty shocked by what she heard. She shook her head and said, 'Only God can help you!'

I told her, 'Babe, God doesn't help people like me!'

Thankfully, she insisted that we try church. The next day we drove to a church in the city. I was okay with the idea of going to church, as I was considering killing myself. I figured, if God was real, he would help me; if not, I would kill myself and at least my wife would have a church group to support her. 'Win-win', I thought.

When I walked into that church, I found something out: God does help people like me. I heard a message of forgiveness, healing, restoration, and most importantly – hope. I hadn't experienced that in my whole life. This message of hope changed my world!

The church was the best place I'd ever been. No fear, no violence, no intimidation. I found a place to be truly myself. I was loved and graciously accepted in spite of my very obvious problems.

In this place, men rallied around me and loved me appropriately for the first time in my life. I discovered total acceptance. I discovered healing. I had role models who were nothing like my dad.

The pastor had a healthy, loving family. He showed me how men should love their wives and children. I lapped it up because I'd never seen this before. I grew in that place as I learned to live a different way of life. I healed in that church and found out what a new start and being a new creation really means.

My pastor became a role model, mentor and spiritual 'dad'. He believed in me, encouraged me and corrected me. He treated me like a son. He saw potential when no-one had ever seen that in me before. That had a huge impact on my life.

I've now been happily married to the same woman for more than 20 years. I have kids of my own. They've never heard their mother sworn at, never seen her punched in the face or thrown across a room. They've never been abused or beaten. They've been raised in a home of love, joy and peace.

Our home is free from addictions and free from shame and guilt. My children are smarter than I ever was, and far more sociable. I look at them every mealtime, grateful to God that I found a different path.

None of this is because I am smart enough to have worked it out, or brilliant enough to have cracked some mysterious code. This is because a supportive community got around my life. It's because strong, godly men showed me how to live and love. It is because we found out that God helps people like me and builds new futures for them.

PART 6
Legacy

Introduction

There we stood on a stage – the three of us: my son, my father and myself – preparing to share at a men's event. Three generations. This was possibly the only time we ever did that.

It was not lost on me how far my family had travelled with the Lord since that moment when Alex Alcorn kneeled down in the gutter in that small country town all those decades ago. That moment of surrender had changed the trajectory of our family line.

So there we were. I was in the middle. Looking to my left, I saw my son. Suddenly it dawned on me: 'Yesterday I was you.' Then I looked to my right and realised, 'Tomorrow I'll be you.' Time travels fast. Since that moment, my father has gone to heaven and my son has become a father himself.

Generations come and generations go. But the biblical blueprint for family is that each generation is enabled, empowered and equipped by the generations that proceeded it; and it is honoured and blessed by the generation that follows it.

The psalmist put it this way:

Praise the LORD.

Blessed are those who fear the LORD,
who find great delight in his commands.

Their children will be mighty in the land;
the generation of the upright will be blessed.

(Psalm 112:1–2)

It is highly probable that the man who wrote that Psalm is David, the shepherd boy who rose to become the king of his nation. This is the biblical record: 'When David was old and full of years, he made his son Solomon king over Israel' (1 Chronicles 23:1).

What occurred beforehand is a lesson for all of us:

David said, 'My son Solomon is young and inexperienced, and the house to be built for the LORD should be of great magnificence and fame and splendour in the sight of all the nations. Therefore I will make preparation for it.' So David made extensive preparations before his death' (1 Chronicles 22:5).

What a life-giving, generation-changing decision: 'I will make preparation for it.'

While I readily acknowledge that very few of us have the capacity to pass such financial wealth on to the following generations, we can be inspired and challenged by the example of David. We have here a father who did not squander his resources in his own lifetime, choosing instead to employ them to set up his son for success in his generation. I wonder whether Solomon was reflecting on his father David's actions when he wrote, 'A good man leaves an inheritance to his children's children' (Proverbs 13:22 NKJV).

Finances and material goods are only part of what we can pass on to our sons. This was highlighted to me one evening when my father and I were both invited to speak after a dinner hosted by a men's group.

After my dad had some fun entertaining the crowd at my expense, I heard him say something I'd never heard from him before: 'Let me tell you about the toughest day in a man's life. It's the day it becomes apparent that your son has overtaken you.'

He went on to make comparisons between his achievements and mine. I fully realise that each statistic he quoted was relative, era by era, but he was setting out to make a point. He continued, 'It's a bitter pill to swallow until you realise your son and all his achievements are the result of investments that you have made in his life over the years.'

Then he delivered his final thought on this matter before walking off stage: 'When you understand that, everything changes. You are no longer competing with the next generation. Instead, you step up to become their greatest cheerleader.'

That gem captures the motivation of every father committed to creating a *healthy legacy*.

23. Pass It On

What will they put on your tombstone? What few words will describe your years on earth? I've already put in my request: 'I told you I was sick!'[1] Pardon me for appearing morbid, but there's a simple reality facing all of us: our mortal lives will one day be over.

A stroll through any cemetery in any city or town bears testimony to that. You'll find plaques on graves, each with the departed's name. That will be accompanied by a date of birth and a date of death, with the two dates separated by a dash.

We live in that dash. It holds within it memories, moments, triumphs, tragedies, joys and sorrows.

Speak to anyone who is in their 80s or 90s and they will tell you how quickly those decades pass. James writes that our life is like 'a mist that appears for a little while and then vanishes' (James 4:14).

The next time you boil water in the kettle, take time to observe the steam it produces. You see it for a moment, then it's gone. It's a graphic image of a human life. Days become years; years quickly become decades. Then it's over – seemingly so fast.

And yet, despite the speed at which the years seem to fly by, we all have opportunities to create a legacy – to leave deposits in the next generation that will live longer than us. A lot of men won't leave a lot of money. But every man can leave pure gold through his personal example.

Despite your start in life, and the disappointments you may have experienced in your past, you have an opportunity to leave your sons and daughters benchmarks for integrity, and memories of sacrifice, loyalty and diligence. Possibly most importantly of all, you can imprint on their minds a model of consistency through a lifetime of loving and caring for your family.

Legacies don't always cost a lot of money, but they never come cheap

In 1924, American canoeist Bill Havens had a choice: compete in the Olympics or witness the birth of his child. Bill chose the latter. Just weeks before the team was due to sail for Paris, Bill was forced to face reality – his baby was due sometime in late July, the exact time at which Bill would be competing thousands of kilometres away.

The decision wasn't an easy one; but Bill gave up his position on the team, and just four days after the games (at which the USA's canoe crew won three gold, one silver and two bronze medals), his son Frank was born.

Roll the calendar forward 28 years, and Bill's son Frank set out for the 1952 Olympic Games in Helsinki. With a time of 57:41, he set a new world record and won the gold medal in the solo 10,000-metre canoeing event. He sent a telegraph to his father afterwards, which read: 'Dear Dad, thanks for waiting around for me to get born in 1924. I'm coming home with the gold medal you should have won. Your loving son, Frank.'

Theologian and academic Elton Trueblood understood this reality: 'A man has made at least a start on discovering the meaning of human life when he plants shade trees under which he knows full well he never will sit.'[2]

When building a legacy, we seldom realise the significance of the small things we're doing. Fathers, your daily actions may not seem much in isolation, but put together over a lifetime, they are sending strong messages and shaping the generation that follows you. Every day you are slowly building a legacy. What we do *this* day will have consequences *one* day.

One of the scariest verses in the Old Testament follows all of the great conquests that came in Joshua's era. It says: 'After that whole generation had been gathered to their ancestors, another generation grew up who knew neither the LORD nor what he had done for Israel' (Judges 2:10). Joshua and his peers are celebrated far and wide for seizing the inheritance that was promised to their ancestors. Their conquests were amazing. But there is one thing that bothers me when I look at the broader context of the Scriptures. The Joshua generation took cities, but they lost the opportunity to give their children a godly legacy.

It makes me wonder how that happened. Were they so consumed with their 'job' that they ignored the tremendous responsibility of leaving a legacy for the next generation through teaching truths to their children? It's challenging.

Noble legacies require intentional activity

In most parts of the world, there has been a rapid decline in children attending programs like Sunday School or Children's Church. There is a generation growing up that knows little about the Lord, his amazing grace, or his miraculous power. The life-giving truths of the Ten Commandments, the Beatitudes and the Lord's Prayer are being lost to a generation, especially if parents don't take seriously their responsibility to teach the next generation these principles at home.

As well as that, too many parents have placed lifestyle ahead of the Bible's call to regularly gather for worship and the teaching of God's word. Something has been lost in the generational transfer. God's pattern has been ignored. No longer is it necessarily true that 'One generation commends your works to another; they tell of your mighty acts' (Psalm 145:4).

We can turn this around, if a generation of fathers will step up to the plate and give leadership to their children through their own example. Building a legacy supersedes building a career, building a share portfolio, or building a reputation as a good guy at the sports club.

Time is ticking. Opportunities need to be taken before your children are grown and out of your home. Create that noble legacy. Show them what it means to be a man of integrity – to be honourable, reliable, generous, consistent, loving and humble.

So what will they say at your funeral? You can start writing your own eulogy today. It's your choice.

24. It's Your Turn Now

There comes a time when we must decide whether we will stay shackled to the pain, neglect or disappointment of the past or move forward – for our own sake, and for the generations that follow.

The Bible encourages us to walk through life 'redeeming the time' (Ephesians 5:16). 'Redeem' means 'buy back'. In ancient civilisations, slaves could be bought back – through being redeemed. You too *can* buy back the years you feel have been stolen from you. There's no better day than today to start that process. I need to ask you an important question: If not now, when? No more procrastination. No more excuses. It's time! You've got nothing to lose.

One of my favourite movies is the Academy Award-winning *Chariots of Fire*. There is a scene in which Harold Abrahams has been beaten, yet again, by the main character of the movie, Eric Liddell. After the race, he's found sitting on his own and feeling sorry for himself. He wants to quit.

As his fiancée approaches him, he declares, 'If I can't win, I won't run.'

She replies, with such truth and insight, 'If you don't run, you can't win!'

So he continues to train and compete, which ultimately earns him an Olympic gold medal.

That's how we succeed. It's not complicated. Get off the sidelines. Quit complaining about how unfair life can be.

Embrace the challenges. And have a go. Give up on the blame game, because that yields no winners.

Even if your own father failed in life and hurt you badly, you won't move forward if you keep blaming him. God knows that. He clearly invites us to let the past go. Listen to him speaking in the Old Testament:

> 'What do you mean when you use this proverb concerning
> the land of Israel, saying:
> "The fathers have eaten sour grapes,
> And the children's teeth are set on edge"?'
> (Ezekiel 18:2 NKJV)

The message in essence is simple: we cannot continue to blame the generations behind us for the way our lives are today. I acknowledge that toxic parental styles are often repeated generationally. But you can make sure that life looks different for your children, and your children's children.

There are important ingredients in the process of changing lives and families. The main one is making decisions. Decisions are powerful. They have consequences. When your life story is told, it won't be your postcode or your genetic code that will have ultimately decided what you became. None of us can change the past, but we can change the future based on decisions we make today.

There was a young person in our youth group many years ago. They were from a disadvantaged, dysfunctional family. It was common for people who grew up in the area to be trapped in cycles of defeat. But if you encountered them today, you would meet a champion: successful in life and happily married with beautiful children.

That all started, decades ago, with a decision to refuse to be trapped in the rut that had defined their parents and the generations before them. They chose to dream of a better future.

There's a price, but it's worth it

We all understand that you get what you pay for in this life. That is something we usually find out by experience. How many times have we grabbed a 'bargain', only to find we wasted our money?

I found this out the hard way. Having always wanted to own a Mini Minor as a young guy, I was thrilled one day to see one for sale on the side of the road for only $600. Bargain? No! That vehicle spent a lot more time being repaired than it ever did being driven, at least while I owned it. I sold that pile of nuts and bolts two years later. Lesson learned: pay the price for things that matter.

The same principle applies to important relationships – for example, your children, your marriage. Invest generously into what really matters.

Like anyone training for a prize, we know we have to keep our eye on the goal, while being prepared to put in the time and effort. Not everything will change quickly. But it will change. That's where *persistence* counts.

During the 1968 Mexico Olympics, a Tanzanian marathon runner became famous not for winning a race, but for finishing it. His name was John Stephen Akhwari. Nineteen kilometres into the 42 km race, he fell to the ground, dislocating his knee and landing heavily on his shoulder. Nevertheless, he got up and kept running, finishing last after the 56 other runners who completed the race.

Akhwari took nearly three-and-a half hours to finish a race that had been won more than an hour earlier. By the time he crossed the finish line, there were only a few thousand people left in the stadium. The small crowd cheered. When an interviewer later asked Akhwari why he kept going, he said, 'My country did not send me 5,000 miles to start the race; they sent me 5,000 miles to finish the race.'[2] May we all have that spirit of determination.

I've met a number of people who have rejected Christianity because they assume it's too restrictive. But if you genuinely seek God, you'll discover that faith is not about what we *can't do*, but all about what God *has done*. It's possible to know the Creator of the universe as your Father.

We can't rewind the clock and start life over again as a child. But we do get a wonderful opportunity to begin a new way of living. It's like being born again. We all have an opportunity to experience that. Stories have a different ending when Jesus is included in the script.

Your story can be different too, if you respond to his voice, and turn to him.

Epilogue

I looked around the auditorium filled with people – young and old, fathers and sons, mothers and daughters, grandchildren, great-grandchildren, and faithful friends. Many more who couldn't be there in person had joined online from all across Australia. They gathered to pay tribute to a man who once sat in a jail cell and thought, 'Not one person in this entire town cares if I live or die.'

Importantly, the bridge between who he was and who he became was *Jesus*!

I looked across the familiar faces – at the great-granddaughters beautifully dressed and the great-grandsons all wearing ties to honour the special man they called 'Old Grandpa'. My heart overflowed with gratitude for God's goodness to our family. We were here to farewell a great man and celebrate his legacy.

The 24-year-old Alex could not have imagined this day on that Sunday night when he went to mock those Christians. Who would have thought that he would leave a legacy that has impacted generations – and has resulted in countless passionate followers of Jesus?

As my sister Francine and I stood on that stage, we had the incredible privilege of telling a little of our father's personal story and how it had produced fruit in us, both now leaders of significant ministries that are reaching people across our nation and beyond.

Then Alex's five grandchildren spoke. All of them were now married, with families of their own. Their admiration for their cheeky, big-hearted patriarch was obvious. As each one took the microphone, love and honour flowed.

'He was the hero that I could reach.'

'He told me that before you become a great man, you first have to be a good man.'

'He had an incredible way of looking at you and seeing you much bigger than you saw yourself.'

'He rang me regularly just to say he loved me.' (They all said that.)

'He prayed for me.'

The common thread was his uncomplicated love for Jesus and people. There was a particular moment during the tributes when it was said of him:

> When he was young, he had to have all his teeth extracted and then wait several weeks for them to make him dentures. I wonder what the people who saw him stagger, drunk and toothless, would say today if they saw the legacy that he's left behind.

I don't like saying goodbye. I'm really not good at it. But there was something very different about the day we honoured my dad. There was a sadness to no longer have my confidante and our patriarch with us anymore, yet I felt incredibly honoured.

Honoured to be my father's son.

On that day in 2021, many things came into focus, but there was none more real than this: we serve the God of generations – the God who introduces himself in the Bible as the God of

Abraham, Isaac and Jacob – and he has a plan for family lines.

David wrote:

One generation shall praise Your works to another, And shall declare Your mighty acts (Psalm 145:4 NKJV).

Many people reading this book may not be happy with their family tree. If that's you, may I leave you with some simple advice? Plant a new one, in the richest soil of all – the unconditional love that flows from the Father heart of God.

A Personal Prayer

Dear God,

I come to you today acknowledging my need of you.

I don't want to continue in my own strength.

I ask you to take from me anything that interferes in my relationship with you. Please forgive my sin.

I know that this is the only way to remove the weight of shame and regret from my life.

I accept you as my Lord and invite you to take me on a healing journey that will bring me to a place of real peace and joy.

From today I call you Father, and I thank you that this is only possible through your Son, Jesus.

Amen.

Notes

Part 1

1 See, for example, Australian Bureau of Statistics, 'Labour Force Status of Families', 18 October 2022, abs.gov.au/statistics/labour/employment-and-unemployment/labour-force-status-families/latest-release#one-parent-families

2 Cassandra Morris, 'This 8-Year-Old Wanted $20 to Give to His Busy Dad', *LittleThings*, 21 July 2015, littlethings.com/family-and-parenting/8-year-old-buys-some-of-dads-time

3 To learn more about how areas of risk for children are related to disengaged and dysfunctional fathering, see The Fathering Project, 'Neglecting to invest in fathers will cost our children their lives', thefatheringproject.org/wp-content/uploads/2022/11/221012_research-doc-3.pdf, p. 3.

4 See Red Frogs Australia, 'What We Do: Supporting the Next Generation', redfrogs.com.au/programs

5 The Fathering Project, 'Behaviour and Delinqency', https://thefathering project.org/why-fathers-matter/

6 The Fathering Project, 'Neglecting to Invest in Fathers Will Cost Our Children Their Lives', thefathering project.org, https://thefatheringproject. org/wp-content/uploads/2022/11/221012_research-doc-3.pdf, p. 3.

Part 2

1 William Lamartine Thompson, 'Softly and Tenderly Jesus is Calling', 1880.

Part 3

1. Italics added.

Part 4

1. Paraphrase of Psalm 100:4 from Eugene H. Peterson, *The Message: The Bible in Contemporary Language*, NavPress, Colorado Springs CO, 2018 [1993].

Part 5

1   Paraphrase of Psalm 116:1–2 from *The Passion Translation*®, Broadstreet® Publishing Group, Savage MN, 2020 [2017].

2   Paraphrase of Proverbs 22:6 from *The Passion Translation*®.

3   Joel Chelliah, *The Chat for Fathers with Sons: Understanding Puberty, Pornography, Sex & Marriage*, Joel Chelliah, 2017.

4   The origins of this quote are found in an essay, 'Social Aims', by Ralph Waldo Emerson, published in 1875.

5   'Saints Among Us: The Work of Mother Teresa', *Time*, vol. 106, no. 26, 29 December 1975.

Part 6

1   These words, quoted on Spike Milligan's tombstone, were first used on the tombstone of BP Roberts, a woman who died in 1970 at age 50 after having been teased about her various imaginary ailments.

2   Trueblood was not the first to make this observation about the meaning of life. Variations of these words have been quoted by many, and date back to ancient times.

3   See Stan Isaacs, 'Bud's Olympiads Are Worth Their Weight in Gold', *Newsday*, 5 November 1991, p. 109).

Acknowledgements

My parents, Alex and Pauline – for whom this book is just another part of the immense legacy of your faithful lives.

My wife, Lyn – your love, support and sacrifice enrich my life.

My sons, Brendan and Ryan – it's an honour to be your dad. The families you are building are the joy of my life.

Grant Thomson – you started this whole thing!

All the team at Acorn Press – thank you for your expertise and especially to Susannah, for calling out the author in me.

The people of Hope Centre – our wonderful church family.

The men who shared their stories – thank you for your honesty, and for allowing your past to be redeemed in order to help others discover a better future.

To the team that worked closely with me – Bek, Daryl-Anne, Christelle, Kirsty, Graham, Luke, Paul, Ryan, Ben, Pete and Indi – for your advice, hard work, proofreading and encouragement.

Each of you have played such an important part in the completion this project. Thank you!

To my Saviour – Jesus Christ, the Father's Son, for all he did to redeem and restore us.

Appendix: Contact Numbers for Support Services

Mensline Australia supports men and boys who are dealing with family and relationship difficulties: phone 1300 789 978 (24 hours), mensline.org.au

Men's Referral Service offers assistance, information and counselling to help men who use family violence: phone 1300 766 491, ntv.org.au/get-help

Beyond Blue provides information and support for anxiety, depression and suicide prevention for everyone in Australia: phone 1300 224 636, beyondblue.org.au

Lifeline has a national number that can give you the contact number for a crisis service in your state: phone 13 11 14 or text 0477 131 114 at night (6pm–midnight AEDT), lifeline.org.au

1800RESPECT is a 24-hour national domestic, family and sexual violence counselling, information and support service for any Australian who has experienced, or is at risk of, family and domestic violence and/or sexual assault: phone 1800 737 732, 1800respect.org.au

Kids Help Line offers telephone and online counselling for young people aged between 5 and 25 in Australia: phone 1800 551 800, email and web counselling at kidshelp.com.au

1800Chaplain is a nationwide toll-free service offering safe and confidential chaplaincy support to everyone, 1800chaplain.com

Circuitbreaker is a program for people who feel that their temper is affecting the quality of their relationships, circuitbreakercourse.net

About the Author

Wayne Alcorn is a son, father and grandfather. Although he was raised in a preacher's home, he had to discover faith and purpose his own way. It's his personal story that makes him relatable to people from all generations and backgrounds.

He is best known for his various leadership roles spanning over 40 years. During that time, he has been a senior pastor of thriving local churches, including the multi-campus Hope Centre. Wayne has taken key leadership roles within the Australian Christian Churches movement, serving as its state president in his home state of Queensland, and from 2009 as its national president.

Wayne's ministry path started in youth work. For almost 20 years, he was involved with Youth Alive in Australia, from the early pioneering phase to leading it nationally – reaching hundreds of thousands of teenagers with a message of hope.

There came a moment in Wayne's life when he realised he'd spent most of his life helping young people, and the time had arrived to help fathers help their children.

Having spent over four decades serving men of all ages in Australia and beyond, he is acutely aware of the challenges facing emerging generations of fathers and sons. He continues to be engaged in programs that effectively transform individuals and communities.

Wayne is much loved as a communicator because of his ability to employ insightful (and humorous) storytelling to amplify biblical truth. Though in demand on platforms both nationally and internationally, it's his private life that keeps him real.

He is energised by his faith, his loving family, time outdoors, fishing on his boat and cheering on (seldom quietly) one of his favourite sporting teams.

Wayne with his dad, Alex, on his 94th birthday, a few weeks before he passed away

Printed in the USA
CPSIA information can be obtained
at www.ICGtesting.com
LVHW011658241223
767353LV00018B/1446